WEALTH CREATION
AND
WEALTH SHARING

WEALTH CREATION

AND

WEALTH SHARING

A Colloquium on Corporate
Governance and Investments in
Human Capital

Margaret M. Blair

THE BROOKINGS INSTITUTION
Washington, D.C.

Copyright © 1996
THE BROOKINGS INSTITUTION
1775 Massachusetts Avenue, N.W., Washington, D.C. 20036

Library of Congress Cataloging-in-Publication data

Blair, Margaret M., 1950-
Wealth creation and wealth sharing : a colloquium on corporate governance and investments in human capital / Margaret M. Blair.
p. cm.
Includes bibliographical references.
ISBN 0-8157-0949-8 (pbk. : alk. Paper)
1. Corporate governance—United States. 2. Corporations—Investor relations—United States. I. Title.
HD2785.8544   1996   96-12531
658.4—dc20   CIP

9 8 7 6 5 4 3 2 1

The paper used in this publication meets the minimum requirements of the American National Standard for Information Sciences-Permanence of Paper for Printed Library Materials, ANSI Z39-48-1984.

Typeset in Times New Roman

Composition by Peter Lindeman, Oakland Street Publishing, Arlington, Va.

Printed by Kirby Lithographic Co., Arlington, Va.

Foreword

Since the mid-1980s, the corporate sector in the United States has been undergoing a fundamental, but still poorly understood, structural change. Corporate profits have been growing rapidly by historic standards, expanding by more than 40 percent in real (inflation-adjusted) terms in the years from 1985 through 1995. The value of stock market equities has grown even faster, with the S&P 500 index, for example, more than doubling in value, in real terms, during the same period.

Although profits at large corporations have risen, their employment has not, and pay for workers has risen less than in previous expansions. In fact, since the mid-1980s, one large corporation after another has announced mass layoffs and downsizing programs. By the mid-1990s the companies that compose the Fortune 500 had nearly 3 million fewer employees than they did in 1985.

To be sure, rising employment at smaller companies more than replaced the jobs eliminated at large corporations. But the new jobs typically paid less. Meanwhile the compensation packages of top corporate executives have increased 50 to 60 percent in real terms since 1985.

Widespread resentment among working people over these developments has emerged as an issue in presidential campaign politics. Politicians in both parties in 1996 suddenly raised questions about whether large corporations were abandoning their social responsibilities to their workers and to the communities where they operate.

What should be the social responsibilities of publicly traded corporations? Anticipating the concern about this question that emerged in the campaign, the Brookings Institution organized a colloquium on corporate governance issues in the summer of 1995. The colloquium focused on the allocation of risks, rewards, and control rights in corporations and on how this allocation is, and ought to be, affected when employees contribute specialized human capital to the enterprise.

Brookings senior fellow Margaret Blair led off the colloquium by presenting a key argument about the social responsibilities of corporations from her award-winning book (published last year by Brookings) *Ownership and Control: Rethinking Corporate Governance for the Twenty-First Century*. Her view is that employees are legitimate stakeholders in corporations, for the same reason that stockholders are—both have invested resources in the success of the company—and that corporate management and directors have an obligation to pay attention to the effects of their decisions on employees as well as on stockholders. Her reasoning is that the specialized investments made by employees in human capital are at risk in corporate activity in ways very similar to that in which equity capital is at risk. Blair acknowledges that the interests of shareholders and of employees often conflict. Managers, who feel obliged to try to balance these interests, face difficult trade-offs. She recommends trying to reduce this conflict by aligning the interests of shareholders and employees through greatly expanded use of equity-based compensation systems.

A group of leading economists, legal scholars, practicing lawyers, shareholder rights activists, business people, and policymakers debated Blair's basic proposition, her analysis of the issues at stake, and her proposed solution. The ensuing discussion raised and examined fundamental questions about the meaning of ownership, the nature and social role of corporations, the responsibilities corporations have to employees, and the legal issues involved in broadening the fiduciary obligations of officers and directors. The participants did not reach consensus on these questions, but they clarified key issues. Blair edited the transcript of that debate to produce this volume.

Blair is grateful to the Alfred P. Sloan Foundation, which provided generous financial support for the colloquium and related activities. She also expresses special appreciation to former Brookings president Bruce MacLaury for hosting the colloquium; to Roswell Perkins of DeBevoise & Plimpton, who served as moderator; and to all of the participants for their thoughtful insights. Blair also thanks Lisa Guillory and Eloise Stinger, who assisted in organizing the conference; Gabriel Loeb for assistance in cleaning up loose ends in the manuscript; Deborah Styles for editing it; and Mark Steese for providing staff assistance. Cynthia Iglesias checked it for factual accuracy.

The views expressed in this volume are those of the colloquium participants and should not be attributed to their organizations or to the trustees, officers, or other staff members of the Brookings Institution.

Michael H. Armacost
President

March 1996
Washington, D.C.

Contents

xi

Conference Participants

M. Bernard Aidinoff
Partner
Sullivan & Cromwell

Amitai Etzioni
Founder
The Communitarian Network
George Washington
University

Martin Ginsburg
Professor of Law
Georgetown University

Oliver Hart
Harvard University

Tony Jackson
New York Bureau Chief
Financial Times (London)

Jonathan Low
Deputy Assistant Secretary
for Work & Technology
Policy
U.S. Department of Labor

Ira Millstein
Senior Partner
Weil, Gotshal & Manges

Roswell Perkins
Partner
DeBevoise & Plimpton

Charles Schultze
Senior Fellow
The Brookings Institution

Sidney G. Winter
Deloitte and Touche
Professor of Management
The Wharton School of the
University of Pennsylvania

Margaret Blair
Senior Fellow
The Brookings Institution

Ronald J. Gilson
Meyers Professor of Law
and Business
Stanford Law School
Stern Professor of Law and
Business
Columbia University School
of Law

Mark Goyder
Director
RSA Inquiry
Tomorrow's Company

Bruce Householder
Executive Director
Worker-Ownership Institute

Bevis Longstreth
Partner
DeBevoise & Plimpton
Adjunct Professor
Columbia University School
of Law

Bruce MacLaury
President Emeritus
The Brookings Institution

Nell Minow
Principal
Lens, Inc.

Charles O. Rossotti
Chairman
American Management
Systems, Inc.

B. Kenneth West
Senior Consultant for
Corporate Governance
TIAA-CREF

Introduction

Bruce MacLaury

The Brookings Institution's interest in corporate governance stems from its legitimate concern with American competitiveness and with the equitable distribution of income and wealth in American society. Corporations are the dominant mechanism by which economic activity is organized in market economies. How corporations perform and whether there are organizational changes that might permit them to perform better is hence an important question for domestic prosperity and for international competitiveness.

The subject warrants attention also because the last decade's flood of restructuring has raised interesting and important questions about ownership and control of corporations, their assets, and their employees. In fact, wherever human capital investment is as important as—or more important than—physical or financial investments—new arrangements for sharing the wealth created by the activities of corporations are emerging. These conditions make questions about wealth creation, wealth sharing, and the social role of corporations timely and important for public policy.

Margaret Blair's book *Ownership and Control: Rethinking Corporate Governance for the Twenty-First Century*, published by Brookings in 1995, provides the intellectual backdrop for this colloquium. Her book is not primarily concerned with whether the chairman of a corporate board ought to be a different person from the CEO, for example. Rather, it raises fundamental questions about the very concept of corporations and the nature of wealth creation.

Blair identifies and classifies a myriad of suggestions for changes in corporate governance structures in the narrower sense of that term. But her real purpose is to lay bare the differing and often conflicting conceptual frameworks that generate conflicting prescriptions for change. It really does matter whether one thinks that corporate performance could be improved best by giving shareholders more voice, by aligning management's interests more closely with those of shareholders, or by muting the voice of shareholders to give management the opportunity to think and manage for the longer term. Those are conflicting conceptions.

The goal of this colloquium is to pick up where Blair's book leaves off. Let me offer some background so we do not get bogged down attacking things that she is not saying. She is not saying that shareholders are not entitled to the stream of profits from corporations in their capacity as investors. She is challenging the casual use of the word "owner" in describing shareholders and asking whether other investors—particularly employees—have also made firm-specific investments that are at risk. She is asking whether those investments also need to be recognized and protected through equity participation, for example, perhaps in exchange for salary reductions.

Second, she is not just rehashing the old debate about the responsibilities of directors to stakeholders other than shareholders, though that issue is, obviously, involved.

Third, she is not asking whether private wealth creation is different from social wealth creation, important though that question may be. She is focusing only on private wealth creation by firms and how that can be maximized.

Fourth, she is not talking about the social responsibilities of corporations, at least not in the vague and broad way in which this subject has often been approached in the past. That is a different subject for a different discussion.

Finally, she is not talking about employee representation on boards of directors, although that is not ruled out.

Too often, discussions of corporate governance resemble dialogs of the deaf—preconceptions are so firmly held as to rule out reasoned thought and debate. The objective of this conference volume is to record thoughtful reactions to new ways of thinking about the changing role of corporations in American society. The growing gap between winners and losers in lifetime incomes, the continuing human (and human capital) costs of wholesale corporate restructurings, and the related emphasis on knowledge-based industries all call for a reassessment of compensation for investments at risk in American corporations.

Laying Out the Problem

Discussion by Margaret Blair

Roswell Perkins (moderator): We have seen in the past decade a truly remarkable reaffirmation of the strengths of an economy based on individual incentives. But individual incentives are not the only factors at work in our economy. To a great extent, we have entrusted the operation of the free enterprise system to the engines and vehicles that we call corporations. Corporations have such an enormous influence on the fabric of our lives that the nature of the corporation and its components deserve continuing intense examination.

Dr. Blair has scrutinized all the literature and put together a panoramic view of the corporation in her book. In addition, she has put forth some theories and theses that we are here to evaluate. So I will ask her to lead us into the play.

Margaret Blair: I have argued elsewhere, both in my book and in an earlier piece I wrote for the *Brookings Review*, that the words "owner" and "ownership" are very misleading words to use in the context of corporate governance questions.[1] Judging by the letters we got after that article came out, I think I must have touched a nerve with that argument. So I will begin with that sensitive issue today. I want to do this by issuing a challenge to the panel as well as to other participants in this colloquium.

The challenge is this. Let's ban the use of the words "owner" and "ownership" in today's conversation, unless we are specifically talking about what these words mean. Let me explain my concern about these words. We commonly hear the argument that shareholders should have certain rights or should be given access to certain powers or processes or that managers or directors should do certain things to enhance share value.

The reason often given is that shareholders are the "owners." We heard this kind of argument recently, for example, in the flap over Kirk Kerkorian's investment in and proposals for change at Chrysler. Kerkorian supporters argued at first that shareholders should be allowed to vote about what to do with Chrysler's large reserve fund of liquid assets because shareholders, after all, are the owners.

But the use of the word in this way illustrates the semantic trap I want to avoid in today's discussion. Asserting that shareholders should have certain control rights because they are the owners is a way of cutting off debate. It assumes that we know the answer to the important questions that I want to talk about at this forum.

The questions are: Who *should* be assigned what control rights, and why?

Instead of using language that implies that we already know the answer, I would like to talk about the contractual roles that shareholders, as well as other corporate participants, play. The contractual role that shareholders play in the complex network of relationships that make up a corporation is that of residual claimant. Shareholders are supposed to get what is left over after all the bills have been paid. It is the fact that shareholders are in the residual claim position, not the fact that in casual parlance we call them owners, that provides the economic and moral rationale for giving them certain residual control rights.

This may sound like a purely semantic point, but it has important substantive implications. We cannot think clearly about corporate governance questions if we start by asserting that one party or another is the "owner." Instead, we must start by asking which parties in the corporate enterprise are contributing what resources and which ones are bearing what risks. We might also ask whether the current allocation of rewards and risks is inevitable for some reason or whether it is an artifact of the contractual design we are using and could be changed.

We also need to know who has de facto control over what information and what decisions and whether those could or should be changed. When you do the analysis in this way, it becomes obvious that in most corporate enterprises the arguments that are used to justify assigning residual control rights to shareholders and calling them "owners" provide an equally legitimate rationale for assigning important residual control rights to other parties in the enterprise.

Why is that? Why should anyone, other than shareholders, have residual control rights in a publicly traded corporation? The reason is that in most modern corporations parties other than shareholders have made firm-specific investments. Those investments are at risk in a way that is almost exactly parallel to the way that equity capital is at risk. For purposes

of discussion today, I am going to focus on one group of such
parties, those who have invested in firm-specific human capital; in other words, the employees.

By firm-specific human capital I mean skills or knowledge or networks of personal relationships that are specialized to a given enterprise and that are more valuable in that
enterprise than they would be in alternative uses. Unlike
generic human capital skills that I could take with me to
another job or another firm, firm-specific human capital
comprises skills that I have or routines or relationships that I
have developed that are of much less value outside the service
of a particular employer.

We cannot measure investments in firm-specific human
capital very precisely, of course. But labor economists tell us
that there is strong reason to believe that firm-specific human
capital is actually quite an important component of most of
the productive activity that takes place within corporations.
For example, economist Robert Topel at the University of
Chicago estimates that as much as 10 to 15 percent of the
total compensation of employees of large corporations is
compensation for firm-specific skills rather than payments
for generic skills. One piece of evidence that we have for this
is that when employees are laid off through no fault of their
own, they take, on average, a 10 to 15 percent cut in pay when
they are re-employed. For employees with ten years or more
of experience with a given employer, the percentage pay cut
is much higher on average.[2] Keep these numbers in mind
because I am going to come back to them in a minute.

Another thing that labor economists tell us about firm-
specific human capital is that, under the terms of the standard
employment contract in the United States, investments in
firm-specific human capital are typically rewarded by

promises to pay employees more than they could make in alternative employment. Sometimes such promises are explicit; more often they are implicit. The employee expects to earn more by staying with the same firm over time and accumulating firm-specific knowledge and skills because he or she sees that other people have earned more when they stayed with the same employer over an extended period of time.

We have an enormous amount of empirical evidence to support this. Firms are able to pay their employees higher wages for firm-specific investments because they share the "rents" or the real economic surplus that is generated by the productive activities of the firm, to which employees contribute.

Under the typical employment contract, employees are paid at a fixed rate. This means that the total economic rents being generated by the firm are typically divided into at least two parts.[3] Employees capture one part in the form of fixed wages or good benefits that are higher than what they could earn in alternative employment (at least in the short run). What is left over after the accounting costs are paid is called the profits. That part is what goes to shareholders.

This may seem confusing. I started out talking about corporate governance and ownership and here I am talking about labor relations and employment contracts. What do these have to do with corporate governance?

The answer is that under the terms of the typical employment contract used in this country, employees with firm-specific skills are, in fact, residual claimants, just as shareholders are. Hence all of the same arguments that have been used to justify running corporations in the interests of shareholders could—in theory, at least—also be used to argue that companies should be run in the interests of employees.

Let me walk through these arguments; they are probably not obvious.

The first thing we have to understand is that corporate profits, as measured by standard accounting rules, provide a very incomplete measure of the total economic surplus generated by corporations. As we have seen, a large part of the total surplus is paid out to employees in the form of higher wages; but the employees' share of the economic surplus, when paid out in this form, is treated as a cost of operation. If Topel's estimates are in the right ballpark, at least ten percent of total employee compensation is not actually a cost in an economic sense; it is part of the wealth being generated by the corporate sector.

To put this into perspective, I note that ten percent of the total compensation paid to employees by corporations from 1990 through 1993 was about $850 billion. This compares with corporate profits during those years, measured in the standard accounting way, of about $991 billion.[4] In other words, what we call corporate profits measures only about half of the total economic surplus being generated by corporations. The other half is typically paid out to employees.

Ordinarily the claim that employees have on the economic surplus takes precedence over the claim that shareholders have, which is why we think of shareholders and not employees as a residual claimant.

But if the company is under financial pressure, employees can be laid off. Under the terms of typical employment agreements, the high wages promised to employees are not truly fixed, nor are they normally a legally enforceable obligation like the interest on corporate debt. Over time, the high wages promised to employees are dependent on the continued ability of the enterprise to generate enough in rents both to pay the high wages promised to employees and to provide a return to shareholders.

Hence employees with firm-specific skills not only share in the real economic residual of the firm; they also, necessarily, share in the residual risk associated with the firm. If Topel's estimates are even close, the value of the rents that employees have at risk in the typical large corporation is, in the aggregate, roughly the same order of magnitude as the value of the stake that shareholders have.

Moreover, because employees' investments and shareholders' investments are often "cospecialized" in the firm, the earnings of employees can generally be enhanced at the expense of shareholders or vice versa.[5] This tradeoff has become really apparent in recent years. Stock prices seem to rise at companies whenever companies announce a new round of corporate downsizings, and stock prices fall at other companies that fail to win wage concessions from their unions.

The fact of this tradeoff makes a mockery of the huge literature that purports to measure the economic benefits provided by corporate activity, or the effect of takeovers or of changes in certain corporate governance arrangements, by measuring only what happens to the stock prices of firms involved in these events.[6]

Even if stock prices accurately measure the capitalized value of corporate profits, they still measure only about half the real wealth being generated by corporate activity, and maybe less than that. Moreover, the half that is reflected in stock prices can often can be enlarged at the expense of the other half.

So, clearly, labor relations practices matter to corporate governance, at least in theory. But in practice, shouldn't it be in the long-run best interest of shareholders to support corporate policies that foster and protect investments in human capital?

To the extent that shareholders capture the returns from those investments, the answer is, of course, yes. But a major point of my argument so far is that shareholders do not capture all of the returns from investments in human capital. Instead, employees share in those returns, and over time they must share in those returns if they are to continue to be motivated to acquire firm-specific skills.

But when accountants record the entire package of payments to employees as a cost, shareholders see the return to employees for their firm-specific investments as something the firms should be trying to cut.

Firms that focus solely on share value will have an incentive to shut down operations that are not generating profits for shareholders even though those operations may still be generating substantial real economic rents. From the point of view of society at large, this is, obviously, inefficient. Moreover, over time such policies are likely to discourage further investments by employees in firm-specific human capital.

For these reasons I believe that a large part of the discussions about corporate governance that have filled the finance and law journals and the business press in recent years has been misguided. The main points of contention have been how to put into place institutional arrangements that maximize value for shareholders and whether shareholders are short-sighted or care only about short-run value at the expense of long-run value.

The problem that I am raising is of a completely different nature and more fundamental. It is about whether maximizing share value, in either the short run or the long run, always maximizes social wealth. My answer is that, under the prevailing labor relations practices in this country, maximizing share value is a dangerously incomplete performance standard for corporations.

I want to anticipate two objections that have been raised to my work and try to answer them.

First, a number of people have heard or seen parts of what I have been working on. They have jumped to the conclusion that I am arguing for an old-fashioned stakeholder model of corporate governance in which corporate managements and directors are viewed as having broadly defined but vague social responsibilities to operate their firms in the interest of society at large. That is not what I am arguing, and I want to carefully distinguish my work from that old model.

Instead, I am arguing that in any given firm there are likely to be a number of parties, in addition to shareholders, who have made some sort of firm-specific investments in the enterprise. Firm-specific investments of all types are at risk in the same way that equity capital is at risk and for the same reason. That is, the value of those investments ultimately depends on the ability of the enterprise to continue to generate an economic surplus. Because of this, I believe management and directors should focus on maximizing the total wealth-creating potential of the firm, not just on maximizing the value of the stake held by shareholders.

A second objection is that whatever merits my arguments may have in theory, in practice they have one of the same weaknesses as the old stakeholder model. This is because measuring the total wealth or real economic surplus being generated by firms is so difficult. If we can't measure what we are trying to maximize, then for what do we hold managers and directors accountable, and how do we implement a wealth-maximizing goal?

I concede that I don't have a good answer for that objection; at least not one that can be neatly applied in every case. But saying that we should abandon the idea of maximizing wealth because we do not have a good yardstick for measuring it is like saying, let's look for your lost keys in the front yard, where the light is better and the grass isn't as tall, even though we know you lost them in the back yard. If we can begin at least to ask the right questions, we may get closer to some answers. We will find the keys a lot sooner if we put our energies into getting some light in the backyard and cutting down the weeds.

Just to get started in that process, let's imagine the following experiment. Imagine that we waved a magic wand tonight, and when we woke up tomorrow morning, all of the compensation contracts in the corporate sector had been altered in the following way. Corporate employees in the aggregate took a ten percent cut in total fixed compensation with that cut being distributed across the employees in each firm in a way that corresponds, roughly, to investments by each employee in firm-specific skills. For example, long-term employees with highly specialized skills might take the largest cuts in fixed pay.

In addition, imagine that the number of outstanding shares of every corporation had doubled and that all the extra shares were now held in some sort of escrow account for employees. Each employee's share of these newly issued shares would be proportional to the cuts in fixed compensation that he or she experienced.

Let's ignore for now the tax consequences of such a transformation—and think instead about some of the differences such a change would make. Under this new scenario, both the pre-magic-wand shareholders and the employees would, on average, take home about the same amount as they would have gotten under the old arrangement. Employees would now get ten percent less in fixed form, however, and the rest would be in the form of a return on the shares held in escrow for them. The variance of returns for the old shareholders would decline, and the short-term variance in total compensation for employees would increase. At the same time, the long-term variance of employees' returns might actually decline, since their job stability and security would probably improve.

In this new world, accounting profits, measured by the corporation, would be about twice as large on average as they would have been under the pre-magic-wand distribution of corporate equity. More important, accounting costs would come much closer to measuring true economic costs, and accounting profits would come closer to measuring the true economic surplus created by each firm in each year. In this model, maximizing value for shareholders would be a much closer proxy for maximizing total wealth being created.

I am not advocating that all firms should be restructured in this way. Anybody who has been involved in the restructuring of United Airlines into an "employee-owned" company knows that it takes a long time to work through such transformations. It is very complicated. We also don't have very many role models to help employees, management, and outside shareholders learn to operate in companies where half the equity is held by employees. The model is probably not right for every firm in any case, but I suspect that a lot of the new organizational forms and complex contracts and compensations schemes that we are seeing in certain sectors of the economy can be understood as the market's groping and experimenting toward forms that provide better incentives and better accounting for investments in human capital.

The point of the thought experiment is to help us break out of the old models that I believe are inhibiting clear thought and to broaden our discussion about what corporate governance should be about.

Firm-Specific Human Capital: How Important Is It?

Discussion by Charles Schultze

Roswell Perkins: Margaret Blair has stressed the importance of fostering and protecting investments in firm-specific human capital. If investments in firm-specific human capital are so important, corporations must have been doing something right for most of this past century to encourage and protect those investments. Charles Schultze, do you think the corporate sector is doing a bad job in this respect? Is there a problem that needs to be fixed? We would welcome your thoughts.

Charles Schultze: Yes, I think there is a problem that needs to be fixed, but it is much more complicated than simply that corporations are not doing a good job. Let me start with a few words on the importance in a modern economy of maintaining long-term attachments between specific workers and specific firms.

As we have already stressed, the first and principal reason for such long-term attachments is that employees gradu-

17

ally acquire skills, knowledge, and habits that are valuable to their particular employers and lead to high productivity. But there are other reasons, too: first, by graduating pay scales with seniority, employers can build a corps of long-service workers who find it in their own interest to remain with the firm and to perform satisfactorily; second, for some employees there is a particularly "happy" and productive match between the job and the firm, on the one hand, and the employee on the other. Employees in such fortuitous circumstances end up earning more than they could elsewhere.

Continuity of association between firm and employees directly or indirectly generates a substantial productivity premium. The joint relationship creates an asset, but it is an asset whose value depends on that continuity of association. In particular, the individual worker can't really alienate the asset or sell it because once you break the association the asset disappears.

There are two measures of the importance and value of that asset. Some time ago Robert Hall estimated that 50 percent of the work done in the United States is done by people who can expect to have fifteen years in the same job. If you restrict this survey to the male work force, 50 percent of the work done is done by people who can expect to remain twenty-five years in the same job. So continuity of association is the way we do business in this country.[7]

Moreover, because compensation rises with seniority, the return to those firm-specific assets may be 10 to 14 percent of the wage bill for "permanent" employees, on the basis of the estimates of tenure-related pay developed by Robert Topel that Blair mentioned. For an employee at fifteen years of tenure it is something in the neighborhood of 30 percent of the wage, and at twenty years it is 35 percent of the wage on average. Indeed, Topel's estimates are closely matched by Bureau of Labor Statistics estimates of what happens to the wages of displaced workers when they are involuntarily displaced. Thus employees with eleven to twenty years of seniority lose initially 28 percent of their former wage when they take a new job at another firm.[8]

That does not count the loss from unemployment; it is just the loss in wages represented by the person's taking a new job at another firm. You can get back up to your former wage gradually, but if you are anywhere remotely approaching my age, you never make it back. To the people who lose the wages, it is terribly important.

Let me say something about the problem of dealing with the implicit contractual relationships involved in twenty- or thirty-year associations. In maintaining these long-term relationships, workers and firms are partly at each other's mercy. They can exploit their dependence on each other.

In particular, the typical long-service worker earns far more than his or her next best opportunities at any other firm. Without protection, the employer could exploit that dependence by cutting the wage premiums. The firm can get away with that because it could make a substantial cut, and the worker would still be doing better than he could do at the next best opportunity. But, of course, given the huge uncertainties about the future, it is not feasible to write a long-term contract specifying wage and employment terms five, ten, twenty, or thirty years ahead.

So we have developed, in our society, informal, unwritten understandings, implicit contracts, social conventions governing relationships and determining what is considered fair and appropriate and expected treatment. These implicit contracts are enforced by considerations of long-term reputation on the part of the firm and, importantly, by the force of social norms and conventions. Those rules of the game have to be simple and easily understood. It is virtually impossible for workers to know whether or not any particular wage cut would represent pure exploitation by the employer or a legitimate move to meet increased competition or other external forces.

The underlying implicit contract that we seem to have developed tends to preclude wage cuts. Wages tend to be sticky downward. Adjustment to adverse conditions generally excludes the route of substantial wage cuts. At any one moment in time, the wage is fixed, and the employer makes a decision on hiring and firing, taking that fixed wage as given. Obviously the system isn't perfectly rigid. We all know of recent examples of wage cuts. But fundamentally wages are sticky downward.

The problem is that such social arrangements are not consistent with the welfare of society or of the workers themselves when major adverse and unforeseen circumstances reduce the overall pool of net revenues available to the firm and its workers. When exogenous events reduce the pool of rewards available to capital and labor, we want to keep the firm-specific assets in operation in that firm—workers and capital—as long as those assets earn more than they could in other uses, even though they may earn less than they had in the past. As long as a return that exceeds zero can be paid to a worker's firm-specific skills, the worker is better off than if employment were terminated and output cut. The same is true, obviously, for returns to specific capital assets.

At the same time, once the return falls below the level of the opportunity cost, we don't want to maintain output and employment at the old levels. The current rigid wage contracts will induce employers to downsize work forces prematurely or excessively when unfavorable circumstances cut the overall pool of rewards to be shared. Faced with lower demands for the product and the rigid wage, firms cut output and employment sooner and by more than is optimal.

Even without any exploitation, the current system can cause premature loss of income-producing assets. Substituting profit-sharing arrangements for some or all of that part of the wage that constitutes a return to firm-specific skills and for other benefits of seniority seems, at least to begin with, a highly promising alternative to explore.

But this alternative raises another set of unresolved questions. Let me comment on just one of the problems that would need to be solved in working out alternative compensation and governance arrangements. This is the problem of measuring the value of firm-specific assets held by individual workers. While we have constructed aggregate estimates, we can't work backward from those aggregate estimates to develop estimates for each individual employee. And the distribution of such values has to be terribly wide. You can see that by the fact that there are workers with very long service who, nevertheless, quit and go to other firms—sometimes at even higher pay than they had been getting—which suggests that, in those cases, the value of their generic human capital is far more important than their firm-specific human capital. We know the quit rate is quite low for long-service employees, but, nevertheless, this suggests that there is a big distribution. So how do you handle this fact?

A second question is, If profit-sharing compensation schemes are such a good idea, why aren't they now used more often? Let me suggest a few reasons why we haven't seen more profit-sharing or equity-sharing kinds of arrangements.

The first point is that we have had alternative mechanisms that served the same function. I think there have been a number of economic developments in recent years that have put increased stress on these institutional arrangements in the labor market, however, and the rigid wage contract isn't quite as useful as it used to be. It is great for an economy in which productivity is growing rapidly; it is much more problematic in an economy in which productivity isn't growing so fast.

We have had a sharp slowdown in the rate of productivity growth in the United States over the past twenty years. If productivity and real wage growth are moving along at a nice 2.5 percent a year clip, the absolute loss of living standards from involuntary separation of long-tenured workers is replaced reasonably quickly.

For example, using Topel's numbers, the average worker with fifteen years tenure will take a 25 percent wage loss, initially, on involuntary separation. With 2.5 percent a year growth in real wages and the normal seniority profile at the new firm, the worker is whole after perhaps five years. That is, he is making as much in real terms as he was when he was laid off. So he is whole absolutely, though not relatively, after five years. Whereas at zero productivity growth after five years, the worker's wages are still 11 percent below what he was making in his previous job, and he still has not caught up after ten years. Much slower productivity growth makes the consequences of the rigidity in the system much more serious than it used to be.

The second possibility is that during the past five to eight years, there has been evidence of increased job insecurity, particularly for white collar and college educated workers. On the basis of a study done by several BLS staff members,[9] I calculated the probability of workers with five years of tenure extending that tenure by another five, ten, or fifteen years with the same employer. Under the labor market conditions at the end of the 1970s and early 1980s for college educated workers with five years of tenure, the probability of remaining with the same employer for another ten years was 50 percent; for another fifteen years, it was 40 percent. But by the end of the 1980s and the early 1990s, those probabilities had fallen sharply. The ten-year extension probability appears to have dropped from 50 percent to 30 percent, and the fifteen-year probability from 40 percent to 25 percent. For high school educated workers the ten-year extension probability fell from 41 percent to 33 percent, and the fifteen-year probability from 26 percent to 23 percent.[10]

An economy with high growth in productivity can get by with informal understandings and long-term implicit contracts that include wage rigidity. The question is whether an economy with much slower growth of productivity and with a somewhat greater chance of involuntary layoff can get by with the same sort of arrangements. It may be that we are going to need some changes and that a system that worked pretty well in the past doesn't work quite so well now.

The Meaning of "Ownership"

Discussion by Oliver Hart

Roswell Perkins: Dr. Blair raised questions in her opening remarks about our use of the word "ownership"; but her point might seem a little academic to some of us.

Professor Hart, what is wrong with saying shareholders are the owners of corporations? After all, it is kind of fundamental, and if we don't start there, where should we start in thinking about ownership and control in corporations?

Oliver Hart: Ownership is such a basic issue that one might think economists would have a very well-developed theory of it; but in fact that is not the case. There are two reasons why they do not. Explaining these may also illuminate the notions of residual control rights and residual income rights that Blair has been talking about, and why we use the word residual in this context.

If you read introductory economics textbooks, you will find, usually, some definition of ownership, somewhere. It doesn't usually occupy a very prominent place because nothing much is done with it, but people feel the need to say something about it somewhere because it is so basic. It is usually defined as a bundle of rights. People say that the owner of an asset has the right to use it as he or she wishes, the right to get the income from it, and the right to sell it. And there are more things on this list.

From a theoretical point of view, one of the problems with such a definition is figuring out which of the things in the bundle is most important. Are they all equally important? Do they all have to go together? Why couldn't we have one person holding the control rights, somebody else holding the income rights, and a third person holding the right to sell the thing? That is the kind of question that is raised in the mind of a theorist.

A second reason why economists do not have a well-developed theory of ownership is more complex. In the past twenty years or so economists have backed away from thinking of all transactions as taking place through markets, and they have found that it is useful to think of a lot of transactions in contractual terms—particularly transactions in which there are significant relationships and specific investments. These are the kind of transactions and relationships Blair's book is about.

Let's say two firms make investments that are specific to their relationship. One of them might build a factory next to the other one, for example, because it is going to supply the other firm with some input. It is not that useful to think of future relations between those firms as arising from market transactions; it is better to think of those firms writing long-term contracts to guard against opportunistic behavior and to make sure that each party gets a return on its relationship-specific investments.

But the problem with that characterization is that, in an ideal world where there are no transactions costs and people could write a very elaborate long-term contract governing the terms of their relationship, it is not clear why ownership would matter. What rights does an owner have? For one thing, the right to decide how an asset should be used. But if you have written the perfect long-term contract, you will have said in the contract exactly how every asset in the relationship is going to be used, because that is, probably, going to be an important part of making sure the relationship works well.

The point is that an ideal, comprehensive, long-term contract would specify everything about the quality of the input and the quantity of the input and what should happen in all the many possible eventualities that might require changes in quality and changes in quantity. An ideal, comprehensive contract like this will specify everything that matters economically. So there is nothing left to control.

Suppose, alternatively, that you think about ownership being the right to income. An ideal contract between two firms that have some kind of synergistic venture will specify exactly who should receive what parts of the income from the relationship. The two firms might sign a very complicated profit-sharing agreement, for example: If the profit is π, I get the square root of π, plus one, and you get the rest. Who knows?

In principal-agent models, the optimal profit-sharing or incentive contract can be very complicated and highly nonlinear. In a situation like this, who is the income claimant? All parties to the transaction will be getting some part of the profit.

So in an ideal contracting world, it is hard to make sense of the idea of ownership because it is hard to say who should be controlling things or who should be getting the income from things. All the decisions that are important for the relationship are specified contractually, and all the ways in which income is going to be divided are specified contractually. If everything can be done by contract, it is hard to say why it matters who owns what.

Vertical integration, for example, is all about common ownership of two sequential operations in a production process. But if everything could be done by contract, it wouldn't matter whether the operations were separately owned and managed by two separate firms or whether the firms merged, and one large firm owned both processes. That is another reason why developing a theory of ownership has turned out to be hard.

In the past few years some progress has been made on thinking about these issues. The world that I have just described is, obviously, idealized. It is highly unrealistic because in practice people can't write very elaborate, comprehensive contracts that are capable of anticipating all aspects of a long-term relationship. In reality, people write incomplete contracts. They write contracts with lots of gaps in them. Once you take that into account, you can begin to make sense of the idea of ownership in terms of residual rights. If I am going to buy an input from you, we will write an incomplete contract in which we say things about the quality and the quantity of the input, but lots of things will be left out of the contract; in particular, lots of ways that your machines are going to be used will be left out of the contract.

Then it makes sense to ask, "Who gets to decide about uses of an asset that are not specified in the contract?" In the context of incomplete contracts, ownership becomes important. It is useful to define ownership as follows: The owner of an asset is the one who has the residual rights of control over the asset—that is the right to use the asset in any way that is not specified contractually or that does not violate some law or some custom.

The idea is that we can always specify certain things in a contract. We might specify, for example, that this room should be used in a particular way at this time next week. If we do that, then the use of the room next week has been specified. In that case, Brookings may not be able to decide how to use this room during that period next week because it has contracted away that right.

But, as for how the room is used the week after, well, as long as that hasn't been contracted away to anybody, Brookings, as owner of the room, has the residual right of control over that and can decide how to use the room. Brookings might decide to rent the room to somebody else, in which case the right to control its use during the specified period next week is gone. But before it contracts that right away, Brookings, as owner, has that residual right.

So we distinguish between specific rights—rights that have been specified in a contract—and all the rights that haven't been specified and that reside with the owner.

You can do the same thing with income. I might write a contract with you that says that the first ten dollars of income from this asset will go to you. That is a specific income right that I have given to you. No doubt I get something in return. We say that I have sold that right to you.

But there will be other income that I haven't contracted away: the residual income. If I agree to give you the first ten dollars, and we get twelve dollars, then there are two dollars of residual income. Who gets that? Normally we think of the owner getting that.

Again, it is useful to distinguish between specific income rights that are being contracted away to creditors or other input providers and the residual income rights, the ones that haven't been contracted away. The latter belong to the owners. We have residual control rights and we have residual income rights. Could we conceive of them being held by different people? This brings us back to where I started. Do these rights have to be bundled together? The answer is that they don't. In fact, sometimes they are unbundled.

Let me give you some examples. One example is public companies that have several classes of shares with different voting rights but similar dividend rights. Then the ratio of cash flow rights to voting rights varies across the classes, which is another way of saying that these rights are not being bundled together on a one-to-one basis. Such unbundlings are relatively rare in the United States and the United Kingdom, but they are very common in some other countries.

A second example is joint ventures. Sometimes companies set up a joint venture in which each has 50 percent of the votes, but each doesn't always have 50 percent of the income. They may divide that up in some other way. So, again, there is some sort of unbundling going on there.

A third example would be someone who is on an incentive scheme with a company. It could be a manager; it could be workers. If you are on an incentive scheme, you become a residual claimant of some sort. But you won't necessarily be given votes.

Those are examples where residual claim rights and residual control rights are unbundled. But I think it is important to realize that there are some strong reasons for thinking that in a lot of cases we want to bundle them.[11]

One of the reasons we might think they should be bundled together is very obvious: if you don't bundle them together, you have an externality. If I have the residual control rights and you have the residual income rights, then it is pretty obvious to see that I may sometimes take actions that are going to affect you and won't be in your interest. For example, suppose some profitable investment project comes along. I may not feel like investing in it. I have the control rights, so I get to decide whether the project is undertaken. But who gains from this profitable project? You are one of the big gainers because you have the residual income rights. I may not bother to do it. If the two things were bundled together, I would have a better incentive.

Another example is multiple classes of shares. One of the dangers of such an arrangement is that bad takeover bids can occur. If you have a company where there is a class of shares with lots of votes but not too many cash flow rights, someone could get control of the company by making a tender offer for that class. Say they could get 50 percent of the votes, with less than 50 percent of the dividend rights. In such a situation, a person who plans to use the company's assets in a bad way, a way that will favor him or her but at the expense of other shareholders' interests, may be able to get control by offering a high premium for the voting shares. Meanwhile, somebody else who might be better overall for shareholders might not be able to get control if he or she doesn't have the will or the means for extracting the private benefits of control that the bad bidder would extract.

When you bundle residual claim rights and control rights together, you force someone who gets control to buy up at least 50 percent of the dividend rights. That is going to align incentives better. So, there are some economic reasons for bundling, but I want to emphasize the point I made a few minutes ago, that bundling is not inevitable.

The next question—and this is really what this conference is about, so at this point I stop—is: Who should have these things? If we have decided that, in a lot of cases, we want to bundle the two things together, we still haven't answered the question: Who should have these bundled residual control and residual income rights? Should it be the people who put up the financial capital—the traditional shareholders—or could it, possibly, be another group like workers or maybe consumers? The answer is that it could be, and we sometimes see that. We see worker-owned companies. We sometimes see consumer cooperatives. So it is possible; it happens.

An important question, which I am sure will come up today, is: Can the market decide this itself? Can we just let firms decide how to set themselves up? If you are setting up a firm, and you want to encourage workers to make relationship-specific investments, you might decide in advance that you will give them some votes. Anyone is free to set up a company in that way, so a big question is: Will the right thing happen automatically through laissez faire, or is there some argument for government intervention or subsidies for particular kinds of companies or whatever?

Rewriting the Contracts

Discussion by Ronald Gilson

Roswell Perkins: The speakers so far have placed a lot of importance on the idea of linking residual control rights to residual risk bearing. Professor Gilson, do you agree with that assessment? If employees are residual risk bearers, along with shareholders, how do we begin to think about dividing up the control rights?

Ronald Gilson: One of the things I have learned from being an academic is that we usually discover things after the rest of the world, not before. The beetles usually figure out what they're supposed to be doing a long time before the entomologists ever come along to tell them why they are doing it.

I think I am the only West Coast representative on the panel. A whole segment of the economy, particularly in the area around Stanford, where I spend a lot of my time, figured out the implications of the human capital issues Blair raises a

long time before the academics started writing about it; and
they are allocating control, residual risk, and residual income
in a complicated variety of ways. If you talk to executives at
a standard venture capital-financed startup company in a
high-technology industry, they won't be surprised by the
notion that workers make firm-specific investments in the
enterprise. They understand that, as a consequence, their
firms need to have some kind of arrangements other than
fixed wage rates, both to provide an incentive and to give the
employees some confidence about their future. By the time
the first or second round of financing goes through, a 50-50
split of the equity between labor and capital isn't unusual.
The outcomes vary, of course, depending on the success of
the company and the success of the industry.

There is nothing in the present governance system—the
system of laws and regulations and background rules—that
gets in the way of people forming enterprises and allocating
control rights in ways that maximize the value of the enterprise. In the context of new startup companies, I don't see
any difference ex ante between maximizing the value of the
enterprise as a whole and maximizing the value of the shareholders' interest. If we look around, we will see that taking
place in myriad different ways reflecting the complexity of
the economy and the character of different industries. Half
the problem, it seems to me, gets solved on a day-to-day
basis, in a rich-textured way, in the ordinary things that business people do.

The other half of the problem is perhaps where the governance, as opposed to the contractual issues, takes a higher
profile. It is in the portion of the economy where we are talking about existing companies, where labor relations take a
more traditional form. Perhaps these companies have a "path

dependency" problem in that they have in place a set of arrangements or understandings that were put into place years, or even decades, ago.

Is there reason to worry that effective adaptation is not going to take place on its own? One of the arguments that gets raised repeatedly is that, as a consequence of the restructurings of the 1980s, through either leveraged transactions or anticipation of leveraged transactions, workers somehow lost the long-term return they had been promised for their firm-specific capital.

I want to take a different view of the empirical facts than that which is behind this argument. To my knowledge there is no significant evidence that on average those transactions caused any substantial drops in blue-collar employment. There is substantial variance from transaction to transaction, but on average, blue-collar employment seemed to be robust to the transactions.

There is a reason for that. You have to distinguish between two different kinds of events that can cause a change in workers' conditions. One is that the shareholder is just behaving opportunistically, saying, "Now I have got this group of employees; I can take some of their return." The other changes result from exogenous events in the economy. The best example is the effect on wage and employment levels of deregulation in the airline industry.

I question whether shareholder opportunism alone is a plausible story. Shareholders could behave opportunistically with respect to one generation of employees. But if in fact firm-specific investment is an important and continuing input for that company, it is not just the existing generation of employees and managers that the shareholders have to deal with; it is the next generation of employees, too. A reputation for cheating one generation will affect the company's ability to deal with the second generation. I am not sure that the scenario of simply a one-time cheating describes a plausible strategy for shareholders in that setting.

Let's consider the second situation, that is, when there has been a large exogenous change that has the effect of devaluing previous inputs. Then, I don't know what the sharing rule, as between shareholders and workers, ought to be.

We do know that if there is an exogenous change that reduces the value of expected cash flows of the corporation, shareholders, clearly, bear some portion of that. The value of the stock goes down. It is plausible that workers will also bear some portion of that decline, through changes in wage rates or changes of employment. I don't think we have any particular way of identifying what that sharing ratio ought to be, which is to say I am not sure we have any evidence that there has been, in effect, a breaching of some commitment with respect to firm-specific capital, rather than, in those settings, simply a reduction in its value. Put differently, I am unconvinced that the existing system is not flexible enough now to allow companies to structure their governance systems along the lines that Blair's analysis demands.

Labor's Multifaceted Role

Discussion by Jonathan Low

Roswell Perkins: I guess we could all agree that human capital in general is a very important input in productive activity. The Department of Labor has been studying technological change in the workplace and high performance work practices. Mr. Low, what can you tell us about the concept of firm-specific human capital and its relationship to corporate performance?

Jonathan Low: The Department of Labor comes to the issue of corporate governance with two sets of responsibilities. One is as steward for ERISA (the Employee Retirement Income Security Act), which oversees the safety and security of workers' pension funds. By our calculation, pension funds governed by ERISA, as of 1994, had about $4.8 trillion in assets under management. This amounts to about 20 percent of all financial assets in the United States. ERISA plans hold about 25 percent of all outstanding equities and account for about 32 percent of the daily trading on the New York Stock Exchange.[12]

There is a tremendous amount of power in these sums, and we (at Labor) have the responsibility of ensuring that those pension funds are prudently managed. And a part of that prudent governance or management is ensuring that the interests of employees as financial investors are properly attended to. At the same time, the Department of Labor is responsible for the health and safety and general working conditions of the American workplace. These two concerns come together in our research into high-performance work-places, the workplaces of the future.

We don't have any final data yet in this research. What we have so far is just a snapshot. But we can certainly share that snapshot with you. The research that we have done sug-gests that there is a relationship between work practices and investments in firm-specific human capital and corporate performance. I don't think that we can yet say that there is causality. Two studies, one by Jeff Kling at MIT and another by Sarah Mavrinac and Neil Jones at Harvard Business School, suggest that there is a relationship between perfor-mance and very specific kinds of practices and inputs like investments in training.[13]

Before I explain that, let me first detour to explain one of the frustrations we have in trying to study this relationship. This is that, with the economy changing from the traditional post-war or twentieth-century structure to a much more dynamic and less well-defined structure, measuring perfor-mance is a huge problem. It's not at all clear that static income statement and balance sheet measures tell us what we want to know. So we are looking for measures that get at the relevant processes or systems involved in success, and these often defy application across companies, industries, sectors, what have you. For the time being we are measuring performance in terms of what we call intermediate outcomes, like changes in quality and in customer retention rates and employee turnover. Using these measures, the evidence suggests that there is a relationship between work practices and intermediate outcomes and that there is also a relationship between these intermediate outcomes and stock price performance and operating and financial performance.

So there does appear to be a relationship between things that look like investments in firm-specific human capital and stock price performance. Does that mean that you can go out and invest in a way that will definitely lead to excess returns or significantly higher performance? We are not sure yet. But, again, the anecdotal evidence suggests that there are people trying to do this. We have been approached at Labor by five different groups that are looking to set up screens or create funds to invest based on these principles.

I would suggest that that sort of dynamic activity in the marketplace is evidence that there may be new ways of increasing the return for pension funds in ways that do not conflict with and may support efforts by management to pay attention to investments in human capital. We feel that we have a responsibility, therefore, to try to examine what the parameters are.

In a similar vein, Wayne Cascio, of the University of Colorado, just completed a study of the effects of massive downsizing.[14] Cascio studied twenty-five firms that had downsized in higher than usual proportions. It appears that the average downsizing in corporate America in the past decade has been at about the 10 percent level. Cascio compared twenty-five firms that had downsized an average of 28 percent with ninety-one other firms in the same industries that had down-sized less than 15 percent. He looked at a seven-year period: three years before the year of the event, the downsizing year, and the three subsequent years, examining the intermediate- and long-term financial effect of these events. He concluded that the downsizing companies did not achieve the efficiencies they had set out to achieve. The data were averaged by year and by industry to provide a benchmark, and the financial per-formance that he looked at was stock price and changes in selling, general and administrative expenses, and earnings before interest, depreciation, and taxes.

Cascio found that, while there was, on average, a 31 per-cent drop in the number of employees over seven years at the downsizing companies, there was a gain of 11.2 percent in selling, general, and administrative expenses and in the costs of goods sold. He also found that, in the three years follow-ing the downsizing event, the companies that downsized had subsequent earnings increases of about 183 percent. However, the comparison firms, which did not downsize, had earnings increases of 422 percent. He also found that the cumulative stock return in the three years following the downsizing for the companies that downsized was 4.7 per-cent; but for the companies that did not downsize, in the same industry, it was 34.3 percent.

We obviously don't know what would have befallen the companies that downsized if they hadn't done so. Perhaps they would have gone out of existence. At the same time, it seems clear that downsizing did not generate great returns over time.

What does this research have to do with corporate gov-ernance?

Downsizing is a tactic adopted in response to a set of economic circumstances. Boards of directors, which, in our view, should be the locus of corporate governance oversight, generally must approve that sort of tactic. We would argue that directors have an obligation to think carefully about such tactics when they are proposed. Traditional nostrums and approaches simply don't always bear out. And pension fund managers, whose job is to get as high a return on their portfolios as is possible without taking undue risks, would be justified in encouraging a second look at such tactics.

The value of this conference is that it can call attention to the implications for investments in human capital of the rapidly changing forces of technology and competition, drawing attention to the need for responsibility and oversight by directors and by institutional investors in regard to corporate practices and policies in this area.

General Discussion

Charles Rossotti: The focus so far has been on firm-specific human capital, but there is also an investment that takes place in generic skills. I am very conscious of this in the business I am in because we are hiring hundreds of people and training them in technology skills. And we are finding that, after we train them, our employees are being hired away at premiums.

The question I want to ask the panel is: What about the buildup in generic skills that is taking place among employees? They are acquiring certain generic skills that are marketable elsewhere, even though they may lose their firm-specific skills if they do market those generic skills elsewhere.

Suppose for example somebody starts at our company, making, let's say, $30,000. Over some period of time they go up to, say, $50,000 a year. This is on the basis of a combination of firm-specific skills that they have acquired and generic skills. Then, if they happen to get in a situation where they can't continue to be employed in our firm, they take a cut to $45,000 a year. What about that $15,000 increment that they have gained by going from $30,000 to $45,000? How does that play into your model?

One of the things that occurs to me is that the employee, as the residual "owner" of his own generic skills, is gaining from investments in human capital. I can tell you that there is a very significant investment in firms like ours in helping employees acquire and increase their generic skills as well as their firm-specific skills. But employees have the right to do whatever they want with them, which in our case generally means jumping ship to go somewhere else across the street for a 15 percent increase.

Margaret Blair: There is an interesting issue underlying your question about who it is that is making the investment as employees accumulate human capital of any type. It obviously complicates the set of issues that I am talking about here. Labor theorists tell us that employees should have some incentive to make the investment in generic skills on their own because those skills are going to be valuable to them somewhere else. You point out that the employees were on the job when they accumulated these skills. The question is: Does being on that particular job reward them as much as they might have been making somewhere else? Were they, in effect, working at less than their potential market wage while they were accumulating those skills? And if, in fact, they turn around and jump to some place else for a higher wage, that suggests to me that perhaps they were. If they are jumping ship, it means that they have an opportunity cost that is higher than what they are getting paid, and so the market signal is correct. They were, in effect, making some of the investment themselves.

Charles Rossotti: And the employees are the ones who "own" those investments?

Margaret Blair: Yes, of course. At least in the sense that they have de facto residual control rights over the use of those investments. That is not, necessarily, a very satisfying answer, and I think that one of the things that complicates this issue is this: In some ways investments in human capital are very similar to investments in physical capital, and in some ways they are very, very different. Trying to think about the allocation of risk and returns, in the context of these complications, is not an easy subject.

The question of who makes the investments is tricky. But it is one of the reasons why we really need to think about equity-based compensation a lot more seriously than we have to date. Firms whose most important assets are human capital need compensation systems that, in effect, ask employees to come on board and to accumulate skills and to participate in the firm. Employees are going to get some fixed wage for doing so, but they are also going to get a significant amount of equity. There are all kinds of reasons why such compensation systems can encourage commitment on the part of employees, particularly if they are paid in restricted stock, for example, and they have to stay for a period of time before they can get its full benefits.

Sidney Winter: We have talked about this word "ownership" in terms principally of control rights, the right to sell, and income rights. When we are speaking of corporations, the right to sell seems to be a rather ambiguous concept. We can take, as a recent example, IBM's acquisition of Lotus. The stockholders and the board of directors of Lotus, apparently, decided to sell the company to IBM. But, of course, they are not in any realistic position to sell the company. They can sell the physical assets, or the patents and whatnot, but they can't sell to IBM the dedication of Lotus's work force.

I would really like to organize a pool about the outcome of this deal. My guess is that IBM will prove to have made a serious mistake this time, as it did in its Rolm acquisition of years past.[15] The reason they made a mistake is precisely that the "owners"—those who have the right to sell Lotus stock— simply have no implements with which to convey the bundle of going concern values and the human capital that is invested in that organization. It is amazing that the market for mergers and acquisitions goes along on the cheerful assumption that you can buy and sell companies. Not so clear. What seems likely is that, eventually, buyers in these situations will catch on, and they will be much more interested in the question of how much of the company actually gets conveyed in the deal. For that purpose, different corporate governance arrangements, which gave more weight to the rights of key holders of firm-specific assets, might actually be helpful.

Ronald Gilson: I don't think it comes as any surprise that a bill of sale can't transfer a portion of the assets. But that doesn't mean that over time some fairly sophisticated ways have not been developed to allow an employee in the setting, for example, of Lotus to effectively transfer his or her good will to the acquiring company. Martin Ginsburg was involved in one of the original transactions that faced this issue when General Motors bought EDS.[16] There was a very carefully crafted structure to effectuate that transaction and to give employees an incentive to make that transfer.

Old-fashioned transactional practice won't cope with the

problem that you describe, but my prediction is that a set of incentives will be provided to the people inside Lotus who are important to IBM. These incentives will be, in effect, a method of allowing those particular employees to capitalize on their value and effectively transfer it.

Martin Ginsburg: Ron Gilson is precisely right. The entire structure of the EDS-General Motors transaction, the use of "class E" stock, the stock appreciation rights, and the Lord knows how much else, was put together solely to convey the work force.[17]

Amitai Etzioni: I am still not clear whether you are talking about efficiency or justice or if you are talking about justice using the words of efficiency.

Let me just add a sentence or two to the question. I am banned from using the word "owner," so let me talk about the people who put in the non-human capital. I guess the traditional story is that they hire themselves some managers, and they make arrangements with the other constituencies to keep them working efficiently: workers, creditors, and consumers. If that doesn't play, then, theoretically, the corporation can get different managers or it will be driven out of business by other corporations that make the arrangements efficiently.

From that viewpoint, I don't understand what the discussion is all about, other than that the market is not doing its thing. If it is justice at issue, are you simply talking about transferring some rights to the workers?

Margaret Blair: That is certainly a fair question: Am I talking about justice, or am I talking about efficiency? While my intention is to talk about efficiency, in some cases, at least in the short run, I am really talking about justice. But if justice doesn't prevail, then in the long run efficiency is harmed, and that is the real issue that I am going for.

One of the short-run efficiency questions is the issue suggested by Charlie Schultze, that with fixed wages as the standard labor market practice and firms focused on maximizing share value, there will be a tendency to lay people off prematurely when the total rents from an activity decline.

The justice question is about situations in which the pool of rents is fixed, but share-value maximizing managers institute restructurings, layoffs, or other policies that have the effect of making shareholders better off simply by expropriating rents from employees. But even here, there is also an efficiency question.

If the market is operating in such a way that employees who have something at risk in the enterprise are vulnerable to such expropriation, they will soon discover that they are vulnerable, that the implicit promises really aren't any good any more, that they can't rely on a promise, real or imagined, that they have jobs for life. They don't have the protection that people might have thought that they had for any number of years.

What is going to happen over time—I think Ron Gilson is exactly right—is that we are going to see changes in new companies as they get formed. They are going to be designed in different ways to account for this and to create more formal structures to protect firm-specific human capital.

Another thing that may happen, however, is that we will find changes going on in which firm-specific human capital is used less because of the contracting problems. When we look around at companies and see that they are laying people off and then hiring them back as subcontractors, we can surmise that those companies have decided that that former employee's skills are not, really, firm specific; they are generic, and they might as well transact their business at arm's length. They don't have any particularly compelling reason to be in an employer-employee relationship. This may work fine for some types of tasks. But there may be other tasks where it is really important to build teams of people who develop firm-specific skills and relationships and who are committed to the enterprise. The problem is that, in the effort to achieve efficiencies in the category of tasks that do not require firm-specific skills, we may be undermining the social mechanisms we once had for fostering and protecting firm-specific skills in those tasks where they are still important.

I think we are seeing the economy moving in all different kinds of directions, trying to adjust to these changes that have taken place that have made a lot of the old implicit contracts seem no longer valid. It is not clear to me whether or not those adjustments are efficiency enhancing or whether we are just trying to adjust around a problem because the old mechanism is not working anymore. Some of them may be efficiency enhancing, and some of them may not be.

Jonathan Low: I have just one addition to that, which is that the change in relationships (between workers and employers) is mirrored by changes in the relationships between corporations. We have heard a fair amount lately about the so-called virtual corporation, which might be, at its extreme, one individual who subcontracts virtually everything else and merely facilitates or manages the final product. In fact, the automobile manufacturers in the country are moving to that model to some degree. Suppliers who, in the past, might have provided merely seat covers, or perhaps even seats, are now providing systems that are installed at the auto assembly plant that have a much higher degree of investment sophistication and technology. Throughout the economy, a great degree of experimentation is going on about how to allocate capital efficiently and what one's expertise really is. One might argue that the automobile companies have decided that, within certain limits, their expertise is in the design, assembly, selling, and marketing of cars, not necessarily in the actual manufacture of all the components.

Core Competency

Maximizing Wealth Creation: In Theory and in Practice

Discussion by Margaret Blair and Ira Millstein

Roswell Perkins: Let's consider this concept of maximizing total wealth-creating potential that has been mentioned several times. Dr. Blair, you are not the first person to use this phrase, are you?

Margaret Blair: No, the phrase is not original with me. There are a number of people who have started talking about corporate goals in these terms, among whom is Ira Millstein, who could not be on this panel today, but who sent us a brief discussion, to be read into the record, of what he means by the phrase "wealth creating capacity."

Ira Millstein's written remarks: The corporate objective, which provides a pole star to guide the actions of the board and management, has been variously stated, but is generally agreed to be focused on "enhancing corporate profit and shareholder gain."[18] Too often this is translated into

51

"maximizing shareholder value," and too often so stating the objective can be read as permitting profit and gain today at the expense of profit and gain in the future. Certainly, short-term corporate profit and shareholder gain is easier to measure and less complicated to consider in corporate decision-making and may even be satisfactory to short-term or transient shareholders. But a solely short-term focus may lead to insufficient investments in technology and training, for example, so that future competitiveness is threatened, to the ultimate detriment of the shareholders.

For these reasons, stating the corporate goal solely in terms of maximizing shareholder value is insufficient. A more satisfactory way to state the corporate goal is "maximizing wealth creating potential." To me, this is synonymous with perpetuating the corporation for the benefit of all shareholders by seeking real economic growth over the long term. By using the word "potential," we attempt to take the focus away from the short-term. So stating the objective permits managers and boards to take into consideration all elements of the corporation's wealth-creating capacity—employees, suppliers, and customers, for example—to consider actions that will potentially motivate and improve the performance of those elements and to invest in such actions as will, it is hoped, achieve that potential. The desired result will be wealth creation over the longer term for the ultimate benefit of the shareholders.

This is not to lose sight of the need to benefit shareholders—that remains the pole star—but to clarify and then emphasize the means of doing so. In any event, our concern should be more with a full explanation of the subject than with fixing on one short-hand expression.

Margaret Blair: Mr. Millstein's comments remind me

that there are two ways that people think about the notion of maximizing wealth-creating potential. One view arises out of the belief that there is a difference between maximizing share value in the short run and maximizing the total shareholder return over time. But can those two concepts really be different? Mr. Millstein obviously thinks that they can be different, and so he wants to give boards the authority or the discretion to do things that are good for the shareholders in the long run, even though shareholders may oppose those actions in the short run because they do not understand their own best interests.

That is not the sense in which I want to use the notion of maximizing wealth-creating capacity. I argue that there can be a long-term fundamental conflict between what is good for shareholders and what is good for the other participants in the firm; if corporate managers and directors are going to be able to build wealth creating machines for the economy, they need some discretion to be able to take into account the welfare of these other participants. I am talking about wealth-creating potential in terms of the total real economic surpluses being generated by the economic activity of the firm. The question is, can we focus on trying to maximize that? Can we ensure that managers and directors have the incentive and the discretion that they need to focus on that, even if it may sometimes be to the disadvantage of shareholders?

If managers are focusing on maximizing total wealth-creating potential, can we look for incentive structures that can try to align those interests so that the disparities between what is good for shareholders and what is good for other stakeholders aren't so great? That is why I am interested in the idea of equity-based compensation systems, so that we try to align those interests, rather than continue to have to juggle the two competing interests. But I know there are people on the panel who don't agree with me that those two interests are, necessarily, at odds and that there is any difference between maximizing total wealth-creating potential and maximizing share value.

I would like to hear the panel talk about that and about the extent to which managers and directors already have the discretion that they need. What kind of incentives do they need to ensure that they pursue maximizing total wealth-creating capacity, if that is different from share value maximizing? Does such a goal need to be mandated in the law? Could it be?

Implications of the Wealth-Maximizing Standard in the Law

Discussion by Bevis Longstreth, Mark Goyder, Nell Minow, M. Bernard Aidinoff, and Ronald Gilson

Roswell Perkins: Let's ask Bevis Longstreth to open discussion of the questions Margaret Blair has just raised. What are the parameters of the law as it relates to this concept of maximizing total wealth-creating potential, Mr. Longstreth?

Bevis Longstreth: It seems to me that Blair has attempted to collect and analyze the large body of literature on corporate ownership, control, and governance, and to distill from it a new paradigm of corporate purpose. If it isn't a new paradigm, and if it is simply an enlightened view of a finance model, then it would disappoint me because I think its ambition and reach are much greater than that. But I derive that from trying to study her text. Let me work with what the words in her book say and try to think about the meaning of that in terms of statute, in terms of how corporations are governed by our state laws.

I was uncertain at first as to the meaning of the new standard of performance that was being articulated in the last chapters of the book. In the opening sentence of the first chapter, where this new idea is formulated, Blair defines the role of public policy in the governance of large, publicly traded corporations to be that of providing "a legal and institutional environment that supports the development of efficient governance structures—that is, those that foster the most efficient use of resources to create wealth for society as a whole."[19] Stated that way, the purpose of corporate law is to achieve that broad purpose. I think there would be very little disagreement about that.

Then there is a leap from that proposition to the newly defined proper objective of the corporation to be pursued by management and the board. That objective is, as you have heard already, "the maximizing of the wealth-producing potential of the enterprise."[20]

Here, there is some ambiguity as to what that standard means. Is this proposed standard intended to work a change in the legally defined purpose of a business corporation, which, as stated by the American Law Institute, is to enhance corporate profit and shareholder gain, or, in the words of Harvard Law School Dean Robert Clark, to maximize the value of the company shares; or is it, as Blair herself puts it, "to maximize value for shareholders"?

In the book she says that, under the new standard, management and the board must "consider the effect of important corporate decisions on all of the company's *stakeholders.*" Stakeholders are defined as "all parties who have contributed inputs to the enterprise and who, as a result, have at risk investments that are highly specialized to that enterprise."[21]

Employees are the principal category of stakeholder discussed in the book. But presumably, under that definition, creditors who have extended credit to the enterprise, customers who have purchased its products on warranty, and communities where the operations are conducted would easily fall into this concept because they each may be said to have investments at risk that are specialized to that enterprise—in the case of communities, for example, public services, schools, parks, air, water, and real estate.

The profit-maximizing norm should not preclude a board, at its option, from considering the effect of its decisions on all these other stakeholders. But new statutory language would be needed, I believe, to achieve a requirement of such consideration—which is what the text says.

With the notion that directors be required to consider all stakeholder interests, then, one can start to appreciate that Blair is, indeed, proposing a change in corporate law and not just a change in the way in which managers act under corporate law as it presently exists. Another statement in this part of the book makes this even clearer. She says: "Boards must understand that they are the representatives of *all* the important stakeholders in the firm—all those whose investments in physical or human capital are at risk."[22]

Under corporate law today, directors owe fiduciary duties of care and loyalty to shareholders alone. All of the other relationships are defined by contract or tort law or governmental law. But the fiduciary duty is owed to shareholders alone, and I don't think there would be a whole lot of disagreement on that point of law, as the law is today. So for directors to become representatives of other stakeholders, a statutory change in fiduciary alignment is needed.

duty of care vs. loyalty   The duty of care could rather easily be adapted to a broader group of claimants. The duty of loyalty, however, is more difficult. Indeed, it is hard to see how a director could act with undivided loyalty to one group of stakeholders without acting disloyally or at least with diminished loyalty to another. The conflict of interests in the allocation of corporate wealth between shareholders and employees, or between creditors and the community, to take two obvious examples, can't be easily fudged.

There is, however, one important body of law—at least one—where the duty of loyalty has been adapted to serve *trust law* multiple and conflicting interests, and that is the law of trust, which has long dealt with the problem that confronts a trustee who is duty bound to serve all beneficiaries of the trust with undivided loyalty. That is what the law says. An income beneficiary, for example, would prefer that trust income be maximized at the expense of capital growth, but the remaining beneficiaries might prefer the trust to emphasize capital growth, which often means reducing trust income. The law has dealt with this. The law has created a duty to deal impartially with the various beneficiaries. The trustee must seek to balance the diverse interests in a manner fair to all.

Thus, as a conceptual matter of law, there is a strong historical precedent for doing what I take it Blair is suggesting, *applying trust laws to corp laws* which is to accommodate the duty of loyalty to serve beneficiaries with differing interests.

And, although the differing interests of stakeholders in a corporate sense may be much wider and more complex than in a normal trust relationship, when the trust instrument allows for invasions of principal for various purposes, discharging the duty of impartiality in the trust context can get complicated and complex, too.

As a matter of policy, you can easily question—and I do question—the idea of granting a board the discretion necessary to discharge this duty of impartiality among various corporate stakeholders. As has been recognized in trust law, the trustee has to be afforded enormous discretion in order to carry out the duty. That means that, as long as the trustee acts in good faith and within some broad realm of reason, it is going to be very hard for beneficiaries or a court to bring a challenge. As a practical matter, I think, to create this kind of duty to a broad set of stakeholders in the corporate context would dilute accountability to the vanishing point. If the relative needs of different stakeholders could be considered as they are in the trust context, supporting greater salaries and retirement benefits or voluntary capital expenditures to ensure clean air and water at a plant site, each at the expense of dividends and capital growth, could readily be justified. If this discretion is exercised with the flexibility accorded by the business judgment rule, then the results will likely become unmeasurable in any useful or practical sense.

Under corporate law as we presently conceive it, the crucial difference between the duties of management to shareholders on the one hand and to other stakeholders on the other hand is the open-ended character of management's duty to shareholders, as sole claimants to the residual value of the firm. Management has a continuing and virtually inexhaustible obligation to its shareholders to increase the residual value of the corporation, rather than to increase the wealth of any other group of stakeholders, and that is the fundamental difference between the claims of other stakeholders and the claims of the shareholders to the board's decisions. Management's duty to the other stakeholders is finite, defined by contract, the law of torts, or governmental rules, and needs simply to be satisfied.[23]

To change that is to introduce the idea that it is okay to create a residual kind of wealth for stakeholders other than shareholders. Indeed, that it is one's duty to be fair. Blair's new corporate goal of wealth creation for the enterprise as a whole, to be parceled out to stakeholders by management with an eye faithful to them all, is very different from our present system.

The law could be written to accommodate this new paradigm; but the policy question that the panel will, I hope, get to is whether it is desirable and whether it would achieve Blair's goals as well as the objective we all agree is behind government's interfering with the private ordering of corporations. This is to increase the welfare of the society as a whole.

It isn't clear in the book whether the new paradigm, if I am getting it at all right, is proposed as a substitute or as an alternative for what we have now. I would strongly hope that what is being discussed here is an alternative.

We have lots of different models for enterprise organization, including general partnerships, limited partnerships, and others. We have mutual insurance companies and mutual banks where the fiduciary duty of directors is to the customer. There are no shareholders. We have limited partnerships where ownership and control are divided by statute, rather sharply. It would make sense, in an open and highly experimental and entrepreneurial society, to allow for other variations. Run them up the flagpole and see what happens. It would be fascinating, for example, to consider the premium that would be charged for capital invested in a corporation that had clearly stated this broader sense of fiduciary duty of directors and management owed to stakeholders. But I would have serious misgivings if this multi-stakeholder model is intended to be a substitute for the model in which directors have fiduciary duties to shareholders only.

Roswell Perkins: Mark Goyder, what is going on in England in regard to this question?

Mark Goyder: The Royal Society for the Encouragement of Arts, Manufactures and Commerce just produced the results of a three-year project with a group of chief executives of UK companies.[24] Our starting point with our group of business leaders was this: What is going to make our companies more competitive?

Very quickly, people were telling us, "We are in a world where people in relationships are the key." What is it that we have to do to be successful in this world? In thinking about this, we are beginning to push the boundaries of the traditional concept of the corporation, this property view of the corporation. This relates to the point made earlier about how to tie up the assets in Lotus.

When we started talking about the legal point, it seemed to the group of CEOs participating in our project that what was absolutely crucial was something that they felt they didn't fully understand until our legal advisor spelled it out for them: under the UK law, the fiduciary accountability is to the company, not to the shareholders. I don't know whether this is because of a difference in law or because of the difference in the way we talk, but Mr. Longstreth was saying that he thought there would be little disagreement about his assertion that, in the United States, the fiduciary duty is owed to shareholders alone. Well, at least in the United Kingdom, the accountability is of a different kind.

If in fact the first accountability is owed to the company, and fiduciary duty is, in some sense, a subset of that, it seems to me that we are very much closer to squaring the kind of circle that this seminar is all about. If the accountability is owed to the company, one then starts to say that the long-term, wealth-creating potential of the company, surely, is what directors are trying to achieve for the shareholders. If, in fact, there is a conflict between the long-term interests of the company and the immediate interest of shareholders, then, yes, indeed, that is the area about which we should be worried; and situations like takeovers clearly are the sharpest manifestations of that.

But the second point our group particularly wanted to emphasize was: How can you fulfill your obligation to the shareholders in a world where people in relationships are the key? How can you fulfill that obligation unless you have in place commitments to your relationships, and a range of measures to protect those commitments, with your suppliers, with your employees, indeed with your community from which you have a kind of informal license to operate? How can you fulfill your fiduciary duty to your shareholders unless you actually know the opportunity costs of all the steps you might be taking in all those relationships?

Therefore, the other rather surprising conclusion that our group came to was that you could actually be, in UK terms, in breach of your fiduciary duty, if you fail to organize your company on the basis that all of these relationships are important because all of these relationships are a source of value to the company.

I have one classic example. Representatives of the company B & Q, a retailer, told us that they engaged in an environmentally friendly policy in purchasing their hardwoods. At first this seemed like just a good thing to do. But at the end of this exercise, they said, "We found a new range of customers that we didn't expect to find, and our accountants are delighted." They could never have justified it in the first place, but after the event they were saying, "This was a very good thing to do for shareholders."

This is a long prelude to a question that I would like to ask the panel from the point of view of our company study: Isn't there a thread we can follow that starts with the concept that the directors' accountability is to the company; and it is in the working through of what is in the long-term interest of the company that we may, actually, be able to find the kind of concept of tomorrow's company in which some of the adversarial claims on them may, in fact, be better reconciled?

Nell Minow: I am very sorry that Steve Wallman, from the Securities and Exchange Commission, isn't here today because he would have said much the same thing that we just heard from Mr. Goyder.

When he makes this point to me, my response to him is, "I agree with you on every part of it except your terminology." I agree that you cannot do your duty to the shareholders, and you certainly cannot do your duty as a corporation, without seriously taking into account all of these other relationships.

At the same time, I will never be comfortable with the terminology that the duty is to the corporation, because I believe that translates into a duty to keeping the current management in place. That is a mistake; they always end up justifying themselves that way.

The big challenge for a corporation is to deal with risk and change, and it is those issues that we want to address. With all these economists here, we could talk about this in terms of maximum efficiency, although other disciplines have other ways of talking about that.

The ideal system would provide the correct incentives and the correct information for maximum efficiency in managing risk and change. One of the examples that Bob Monks and I use in our textbook is this: What color should the wall be painted in the factory? We believe that, in general, the way to decide who within the corporate structure should make this decision—whether it should be the shareholders, the board of directors, the managers, or the employees—boils down to two issues. Who has the best source of information? And who has the fewest conflicts of interest?

It seems that the employees would, probably, be the best ones to decide what color the walls in the factory should be painted, although there might be a range within which they must decide. For example, you wouldn't want to allow them to select gold leaf.

On the question of how often the walls should be painted, perhaps that is not best given to the employees, unless you can make it economically a part of their package, in which case we can say, "Well, you can paint the walls as often as you like, but it will come out of your salary." You might find that the walls never got painted. There comes a point where, as a matter of maintenance, that is probably not in the interest of the corporation or the shareholders.[25]

When I was invited to talk to my son's third-grade class about my book and about being a writer, I explained to them how an editor is like a teacher who marks up your work. They were all very interested.

When I got toward the end, I came to the question I had been dreading, which is, "What is the book about?" I was desperate. Finally, inspiration struck me, and I said, "Is anybody in the room a sports fan?" All the hands went up, and I said, "Has anybody ever heard of the Chicago Cubs?"

"Yes, yes." I am from Chicago myself, so I was glad to see that everybody knew who the Chicago Cubs were, and I said,

"Okay. Does anybody know, what is the one thing that, until recently, every other team could do but the Chicago Cubs could not?" One little boy raised his hand and said, "Field."

Participant: I was going to say, "Win a pennant."

Nell Minow: Win a pennant, right. They are still behind on that one, too, but there is one other thing that they only recently have been able to do, and that is play night games. They couldn't play night games for years because they didn't have lights at Wrigley Field. In 1968, a group of shareholders sued, and they said, "We are the shareholders. When you came to the public markets for money, you promised us that you would do everything you could within the law to give us as much of a return as you could. If we had night games, we would get more ticket revenues. We would get more television revenues. We would get more concession revenues. And maybe the team would learn how to play better, too."

Mr. Wrigley said, "Baseball is an afternoon game." That was not a decision made on the basis of the community; the community could have enacted zoning restrictions if it didn't want people coming in at night. That decision was made because baseball, according to Wrigley, was an afternoon game. Not until the Cubs were owned by someone else did they get lights and were thus able to play night games. We are still waiting for them to win a pennant.

But the point is, who makes that decision? Is it Mr. Wrigley? Or is it the shareholders? Or is it the Cubs themselves? Do we solve the problem by making the team members shareholders?

Let's think about that for a moment. I was on a panel once with a woman from Pepsi, who was talking about their extraordinary program to make every Pepsi employee throughout the world a shareholder.

I asked her, "What has the impact been on the employees? Are they more motivated? Are they doing a better job at Pepsi?"

She laughed and said, "You know, we have not found any impact whatsoever in terms of their incentive to perform better. At the same time, there has been a profound impact on their incentive to consume Pepsi products."

They all went to Pizza Hut. They went to Taco Bell. They ate Fritos. They were the most motivated consumers you can imagine. Isn't it curious that they felt that they had, at some level, more of a chance to affect the share value of the company as consumers than they did as employees?

Another problem concerns certain risks of making employees owners. ESOPs (Employee Stock Ownership Plans), for example, have sometimes been used to entrench management, explicitly as anti-takeover devices. We are involved in a company right now where 37 percent of the stock is owned by the ESOP. The ESOP is managed by the Chase Manhattan Bank. The former vice-chair of Chase is on the company board. It is a very cozy relationship, and we feel that they have not done what most of us would like to see in terms of providing some kind of a market reaction to the company.

Another question I have concerns the management structure. Some people have argued that employee ownership would mean running companies by committee. Blair responds there is no particular reason why employee owners could not agree to set up a hierarchical management structure.

But does that solve the problem? Doesn't it just create a whole new set of agency costs? There needs to be some balance between involving the employees and totally bogging down the company.

The largest pool of equity capital ever in the history of the galaxy as far as anybody knows is, of course, in ERISA-administered pension plans. The ERISA plans could play some of the role that Blair is suggesting here, and I hope they will do that.

But I think it is important to be very company specific as we talk about some of these structural issues. Consider the issue that was raised by the IBM/Lotus example discussed earlier, the issue of the extent to which individual employees really are the company's assets. Consider Saatchi & Saatchi (a publicly traded advertising agency), for example.[26] This was a lovely example of shareholder activism with one small problem, which was that, after it was over, the entire assets of the company walked out the door.

What do you do about a chief executive who is incredibly creative and has very solid client relationships, but who is a lousy businessman? That company has to be private. I would argue the same thing applies to the Chicago Cubs. There would have been no baseball strike last year, believe me, if the sports teams were using equity-based compensation systems. When the company is totally dependent on the individual abilities and the relationships of specific people, this is not a good time to go to the public markets for money. That is why law firms are "employee-owned," so to speak.

The answer to the question may also have an evolutionary aspect—that is, different ownership and governance arrangements may be appropriate at different points in a company's life cycle. My partner, Bob Monks, who is married to a descendant of Andrew Carnegie, often says to me, "How many times did the Rockefeller heirs get paid back for that first $100 investment?" Maybe companies need to evolve somehow from a point when it's appropriate to go to the public markets for money to a point when it's more appropriate to be employee-owned.

M. Bernard Aidinoff: I think we have to acknowledge that our boards of directors do have considerable flexibility and that, as a practical matter, they do take into consideration things other than the maximization of shareholder value. On the one hand, very few situations arise in which corporate directors face such a direct conflict that their judgment will be criticized or will be the subject of litigation. On the other hand, in the really dramatic cases, I don't think that directors really have much alternative to considering what is best for the shareholders. They avoid a lot of the questions and resolve them in favor of long-term value, which sometimes is merely an excuse not really for favoring long-term value but for deciding that some other interest—whether it is environmental or community related—is good for the company.

I assume that Philip Morris supports the arts in order to maximize shareholder value, that they think they get some goodwill value in the community. But I also know that there are organizations and corporations that support the arts for no other reason than that their CEO or their board happens to be interested in the particular community. Whether that is good for shareholders or bad for shareholders, is sort of irrelevant as long as it doesn't go to an extreme, and I think we permit that type of discretion.

At the same time, I have great difficulty with substituting what has been called the wealth-creating potential as a required standard for a board of directors.

As a practical matter, I think that this discussion may be overemphasizing residual value, rather than simply asking what the market requires at the time the investment is made. Sometimes, in order to raise capital for example, preferred stock that pays a huge dividend has to be issued rather than common stock. Management has to look at what restrictions creditors will impose or what conditions are required to attract the type of people you want to work in the company. Boards and managements must weigh the relative bargaining power and do what is necessary either to get the necessary capital or to get and keep the necessary people.

The whole high-tech area has done very, very well for both its shareholders and its employees by giving employees huge stakes in the company, for example. But in many cases, this was done simply because the company didn't have the cash to give as compensation. While one has to be fair to employees, I don't think that they are entitled to anything special at the time of a huge takeover in which a 100 percent premium is offered to the shareholders. I think the shareholders are entitled to that premium, and I think that a board, when faced with such an offer, is going to have great difficulty weighing the other factors. But, presumably, those factors have been taken into account, perhaps in the original contract with the company, which may have given some people higher wages than they might normally have had and may have given them some of the same interests that other shareholders have. The same factors also get taken into account in the negotiations with the company that is doing the takeover. It would be nonsensical for IBM to acquire Lotus, for example, without doing something to ensure that employees of Lotus continue. But if Lotus had concluded that it was not going to accept the offer of IBM, I certainly wouldn't want to be a director of Lotus.

Roswell Perkins: Professor Gilson, can you comment on the scope of the objective of corporations, as stated in the report on corporate governance issued by the American Law Institute? Do you think it is too narrow in the light of all that has been discussed here, or do you think it gives executives enough freedom? As you may recall, it says that the objective of the corporations is the "conduct of business activities with a view to enhancing corporate profit and shareholder gains."[27]

Ronald Gilson: It seems to me that the presentation in that document is really fine. The only circumstance in which one gets concerned about that presentation is if we believe there is a persistent pattern in which market glitches will cause an increase in shareholder gain and corporate value at the expense of other investors in the company. But I don't believe there is any reason to assume that is likely to happen in any significant way. In any case, this formulation leaves people free to structure a relationship that is peculiar to their own circumstances.

Employee Involvement
in Practice

Discussion by Bruce Householder
and Kenneth West

Roswell Perkins: This question of employees being encouraged or persuaded to accept profit sharing or equity sharing is an important one. The Worker-Ownership Institute is a small research and consulting organization created and supported by the United Steel Workers of America and by steel companies. Bruce Householder, I understand your institute is actively promoting corporate reorganizations through the use of ESOPs. Can you tell us about that and what kind of a role worker/owners should have in corporate governance?

Bruce Householder: I come from a company that was bought out by an ESOP, and my experience there and through the Worker-Ownership Institute is that employee ownership requires a change in the attitude and in the environment of the company itself. The right management has to be in place, management that will work with the employees on the floor and with the employees in the salary ranks. The employees

71

have to be involved. But this requires training. Employees need training, for example, in what an ESOP is and what their input into an ESOP means and requires.

In some companies you will find that employees are involved all the way from the floor to the board of directors. They may have seats on boards of directors, which means that they have to be trained in new roles and responsibilities. When employees get to the board room, they find that they have a whole new set of responsibilities other than the issues that they bring up from the floor. Their responsibilities are to the shareholders, whether they are from outside or from within the company. Involving employees and making them shareholders in the company can make a company more profitable. People have to be trained to understand this, but when employees realize that they can create value through their involvement in their company, that they can save money for that company, and that this increases their return as shareholders, they will respond. If they are involved in every step of the company's process and involved with customers, they can give a big boost to the business itself.

Management, from the CEO down to the foreman on the floor, and all the other employees have to have a partnership. If they have that—and a lot of companies certainly do not— they can save a lot of costs. But the people must have input. They must feel important in their role and in their plant. Their job is important to them.

A lot of the ESOPs were formed in the steel industry as a last resort. The plants were in trouble, and the parent companies wanted to unload them. The people in these companies that are now employee owned are driven to survive. They want to prove that they have some value, that they can make their company succeed, and that they add value to that company.

In the long range it may not be feasible for companies to be 100 percent owned by the ESOP because companies have to sell shares in the public market to get capital to improve their company. But the only way that a company can raise capital to build its business is to show that it is functional and profitable. And once the company sells shares in the public market, the employee can see his or her stock every day in the newspaper. The employees feel more involved that way. They can watch the stock price. I think that when they see that, it actually increases their involvement and input. Another important aspect of employee ownership is sharing of business and financial information with employees. Employees want to know what is going on in their companies. They don't want to leave their head at the gate anymore.

In a traditional company, it is a little bit harder to get to that point. A lot of companies have tried to get there, and some have been successful in areas. But I think when you make the employees shareholders, you prop those employees up a little bit, and you make them have pride in the company that they work for.

Kenneth West: In my former life as a CEO, I found that corporate pyramids were drawn upside down. We decided quite a long time ago in our company that the management should be at the bottom. The employees are next, and the customers are king. When you convince the employees that every one of them is involved in the process of attracting and retaining customers, and that there is something in that game for them, some reward system, then you have found magic.

TQM (Total Quality Management) has gotten to be a buzz word now, but I really think there are ways to involve employees and to empower them to do the job. They know what training they need. They know what the customers want. And if you empower them to do their job, then I think a lot of these issues of how you run the corporation and how it is structured kind of go away by themselves.

The structure emerges out of fairness with the employees and empowerment and participation and incentives, all those good words. There are a lot of ways to do that—ESOPs, employee ownership, profit-sharing schemes, or other incentive schemes that you can tailor to each company.

Investments in firm-specific human capital can be encouraged and employees treated fairly, I think, within the existing paradigm. So I agree with Bevis that if there is a new paradigm to be tried, I hope it is an alternative, not a substitute.

I'd like to raise a different problem. I am not sure I understand fully what firm-specific human capital is. The people in our firm, who, to my way of understanding it, have the most firm-specific capital, are the people who are most valuable in the marketplace: they have the core competencies, and the other guys want them. So I don't worry too much about fairness to that particular group of employees with well-developed firm-specific human capital.

General Discussion

Roswell Perkins: I'd like to ask Mr. Aidinoff whether there is any difficulty with the big multinational corporations in having equity-sharing compensation systems.

M. Bernard Aidinoff: Any multinational corporation has the problem of how to adapt to very complex local rules. But it is also clear that, one way or another, depending on what the legal and tax considerations are in the specific countries, appropriate overall benefit plans and stock option plans and restricted stock plans and phantom stock plans and bonus plans can be designed to give the necessary incentives.

Roswell Perkins: I think we have reached a point where we can call for questions from anyone who would like to challenge anything that has been said in the panel.

Tony Jackson: One of the recurring themes here has

been about a kind of contractual imbalance between labor and capital in the sense that the workers have to carry on investing their time, but firms don't guarantee their continuity in the old way, for exogenous reasons that have been touched on. So, in this way, the workers are being shortchanged. It seems to me that stock is one perfectly legitimate way of making good the shortfall.

But I am trying to imagine what the mechanism might be that would make the stockholders cough up. I don't see the fund managers putting pressure on companies to share stock with employees. They're more likely to say, "It is tough for the workers in the modern world, but my responsibility is to the savers who put their money with me."

Legislation to make companies cough up would look a bit like expropriation. Presumably, they would only give up a partial entitlement to an income stream if they genuinely believed that the income stream would, therefore, be so increased that they would end up better off.

Could I specifically ask Nell Minow whether the institutions that she talks to show signs of thinking along those lines? Do they believe in it?

Nell Minow: I think that Jon Low is probably better equipped to answer that than I am, but I think that the work that they have done at the Department of Labor suggests that there are financial consequences from structures that foster and protect investments in human capital and that these are of tremendous appeal to people who are interested in investing.

Jonathan Low: First of all, I think the size of the institutional investor community and the size of the funds they represent make it more difficult for them to do the traditional Wall Street walk. Some of these pension funds are so big, they move the market when they take their money out of a company. Because they no longer have that option, they have to become more involved or more concerned, anyway, about the underlying strength of the company and the securities in which they have invested.

Likewise, many of these funds are indexed, so they have to become concerned because the value and strength of the index depends on the way the companies in the index are managed. Ken West, who has just started advising TIAA-CREF on corporate governance, should probably say a word here, as well.

Kenneth West: My objective with TIAA-CREF is to develop a process to assess and monitor the corporate governance practices of the companies in which TIAA-CREF, but primarily CREF, which is the equity arm of the institution, invests. Jonathan is exactly right. CREF owns approximately $65 to $75 billion of equities. They cannot walk the Wall Street walk. CREF indexes around two-thirds to three-quarters of those portfolios. A large share of the managed part of the portfolio, in addition, comprises companies that are in the indexes. So, like it or not, we are stuck as long-term investors. But the CREF funds have been very responsible long-term investors for many years. They have developed principles of good corporate governance, which have been circulated to all of the portfolio companies.

The idea now is to evaluate all 1,400 or 1,500 companies in that portfolio for their corporate governance policies and practices and to find those that are not adhering to good corporate governance policies and practices as we would define them in the current paradigm and to do something about that.

It is a monumental task because, once you find a company that is not performing well in one of those categories, you can eat up enormous amounts of time and expense in just talking to them. So we have to work out a model to do that.

But the fact is that responsible institutional investors with the help of many people in this field now, I think, are on the track. I think a lot is going on in corporate America in terms of improving its corporate governance practices, again within the current paradigm. I am not talking about a new model that might emerge. But I am very optimistic that great progress has been made over the past ten years in this field, and I think great progress is going to be made in the next ten.

Bruce MacLaury: I would like to make one more attempt at reconciliation or clarification.

We started out this second half by talking about this notion of maximization of wealth-creation potential. And at the beginning of the discussion we were talking about unbundling ownership. I think what Margaret is talking about is unbundling the contribution that employees make. Employees provide their time to a corporation. They provide the application of generic knowledge, and they are also, at the same time, investors in firm-specific knowledge that is of value and generates in itself a stream of income.

What, it seems to me, she is trying to get at is that the method of compensation for these different attributes of employees ought to be different, that for the contribution of time and generic knowledge, you can have salaries and bonuses. Some of it can be variable. It doesn't have to be all fixed, but it is a fixed cost of employment, so to speak.

In their capacities as investors in firm-specific knowledge, employees are at risk in the way that Charlie Schultze was describing. For that element, they ought to be compensated by an equity participation, which pays dividends and the rest. Then, it seems to me, if that is logical, what we should be talking about is not employees versus shareholders. We should be talking about employee shareholders and non-employee shareholders.

If employees have given up some salary in exchange for shares, I am at a loss to understand why there is a difference between the responsibility of a corporate director for maximizing the wealth-creating potential of a corporation, on the one hand, versus maximizing shareholder value on the other.

It seems to me that that reconciles this dilemma that we have been talking about. But, to repeat what I said earlier, a distinction that I think needs to be kept in mind is that we are not talking about maximizing wealth creation potential for society as a whole. We are talking about maximizing wealth creation by a firm, or a corporation. There is a whole separate set of issues about pollution and all the rest, where society has a vested stake but where the corporation may or may not, depending on how it sees its long-term interests.

Charles Schultze: I think the basic proposition of splitting out employee compensation into several components and making one of those components depend on the variable fortunes of the firm, namely, profit sharing, makes a lot of sense for a lot of reasons, and I think it reduces the problem of maximizing wealth creation and conflicting objectives of managers looking at different stakeholders. But it doesn't eliminate the problem. And it presents problems of its own. For example, firm-specific capital owned by workers is quite different from other forms of capital in at least one critical aspect. When the worker leaves the firm, the capital disappears. The worker can't alienate it. By contrast, a stockholder can sell his shares to another stockholder, and the specific machine tool that was bought with my money, in effect, stays in the firm. So, you can't simply hand out stock and say that the worker is a stockholder like other stockholders and has the same interest. The interests are not the same.

Second, there is a difference in risk preferences. At least, it is commonly believed that workers, for good reason, are much less interested in variable returns than stock owners, who can diversify. So on the one hand I agree strongly that there is some real potential for making improvements in the current complicated way we reward owners of different assets, and I think we could reduce a lot of the problem. On the other hand, I think there is a hornet's nest that will require a great deal more research to figure out how to get this done.

Oliver Hart: I have a comment that may help to clarify whether there is a conflict between value creation and maximization of profit or value for shareholders. A useful way to think about this is at the time a company is first set up. A point that is important to realize is that if you are setting up a company, you may at some point want to exit from the company.

Knowing that going in, you would want to create a company that is as valuable as possible because you are going to be selling out to other people. So you are worried about giving workers the right incentives to acquire firm-specific skills. You might at first think that you should give all the control rights to shareholders because you are going to go public and you are going to be issuing shares to non-employees. And you want those shares to be as valuable as possible, so you give the shareholders all the votes. But on the other hand, you are worried that, if you do that, workers won't work very hard, and the company won't be worth very much, and so the shareholders won't pay very much for the shares.

So it turns out that it is not a very attractive option to give all the votes to outside shareholders. You may find it more attractive to set up the company in such a way that the workers have some shares and some votes. That way they are going to have more of an incentive to create value, the company is going to be more profitable, and people will pay more in aggregate to hold the shares of that company. So, as you retire, you will make more money.

That is an example to show that the person who first sets up a company—and that is a rather idealized way of thinking about it—actually does have an incentive to put into position a governance structure that takes into account all these incentive effects on workers, or I could imagine a case in which it is customers to whom it might be desirable to give some rights, as well.

So, I think ex ante, in many cases, there is no conflict between total value creation and value for shareholders because, really, the value for the shareholders is the value for the initial owner, and that is the same as the total value of the company.

Having said that, I think it is incorrect to say there are no conflicts of interest ever, because later on conflicts can develop. A simple example would be if somebody makes a takeover at a handsome premium, which would be very attractive for shareholders or at least for some of them but might be less attractive for the employees, even if they are also shareholders, because perhaps the person taking over the company might be planning to fire a lot of them. So, in that case, there are serious ex post conflicts of interest. I think the kind of thing that Bruce MacLaury was talking about may, indeed, help with that, but it is not going to eliminate it.

I would like to raise a question about the things that Bevis was saying. Just as a matter of fact, I would be interested to know whether there is anything to stop somebody setting up a company now in which they say that the board should have a duty of loyalty not just to shareholders, but to workers as well. If I wanted to set up a company that way and if I wrote that into the corporate charter, is it the case that the courts would respect that if we got into a dispute? Or would they say, "Well, we are not used to that; we are not going to pay any attention to that." Maybe Ron Gilson should answer that, too. It seems to me that if the courts will respect that, then in fact we have the ability right now to set up companies in which fiduciary responsibilities run to employees as well as to shareholders. Certainly, there is no reason why you can't put workers on the board if you want to. If you don't want to, you don't have to.

Another small point is that across countries, it is sometimes quite misleading to look at the definition of fiduciary duty. In the United Kingdom the fiduciary duty is owed to the company. Nonetheless, UK takeover rules, for example, have been much less friendly to management than U.S. takeover rules, even though in the United States the managers seem to have a narrower fiduciary duty to shareholders. In the United Kingdom, with its broader notion of fiduciary responsibilities, it is, nonetheless, much harder for managers, as I understand it, to turn down a takeover on the grounds that it would be in the interest of workers (to turn it down) and not of shareholders.

Bevis Longstreth: I think the answer to the question you asked is that you couldn't, under Delaware statute, for example, redefine the duties of care and loyalty to be owed to a broader class than the corporation and its shareholders. So the law would have to be changed to give this alternative a chance for full expression.

I wanted to say something about a problem that I see with ESOPs in general and what is being proposed here as a way of motivating the employees and bringing them into a position of greater importance to the company through share ownership. It seems to me there are lots of ways of sharing profits, sharing wealth with employees; and share ownership is one way, and that is suggested as a way in the book.

But it seems to me that if I were an individual who was investing increasingly and making firm-specific investments in a firm, to the degree I was doing that, I would want to be paid a share of the profits in cash so that I could diversify my risk through investments of that cash outside the firm, not inside the firm.

So I would propose a rule of logic almost opposite to what Margaret is proposing: that the more firm-specific my investments in the firm were, the less I would be interested in stock ownership. I would still want a share of the profits for my work, but I would want that share in cash so that I could diversify out of the firm against the day that this firm, for whatever technological or other exogenous reason, ceased to be successful.

Ronald Gilson: Let me elaborate briefly on Bevis's answer to Professor Hart's question about how you can set up the company.

I agree with Bevis that there is great uncertainty as to whether one could formally alter the charter to accomplish the broadening of the duty that Professor Hart suggested. The American Law Institute's *Principles of Corporate Governance*

ducks the point.[28] But I think it is fair to say that we duck it
explicitly, rather than letting it slip under the table.

If we say accountability to the company, my concern is
that it is an empty phrase because the company isn't in a position to demand that accountability. Do we have a way of looking at standard U.S. practice and deciding whether the managers meet whatever standard we are talking about? Moreover,
will the court impose liability if the court thinks that the managers haven't met it?

At a second level, can the directors block a takeover
attempt, based on the proposition that the acquiring company
is going to change what they do? Can the managers block a
proxy fight to remove the directors, based on the proposition
that the proponents of the proxy fight mean to change the way
the company is behaving?

But having said that you can't alter the charter directly,
it seems to me that it is really quite easy to do so functional-
ly, once you recognize that when we talk about accountability to something, we must mean accountability to someone.
You can create mechanisms of accountability. Those mechanisms of accountability turn out to be the most significant
thing: *Who* gets to evaluate the extent to which the company
has lived up to whatever duty we impose on them?

So I can create a company that responds to Professor
Hart's concerns because I can make sure that I allocate stock
to the groups to which the company is accountable in one of
these functional senses in a fashion that will allow the members of the group to act. If I want to broaden fiduciary responsibilities to the employees, I can create a class of stock that I
give to the employees, which gives them certain specified
decision rights. I can do that easily.

I can also create a wide variety of incentives and decisionmaking structures within the company without altering the magic phrase. And, likewise, altering the magic phrase without careful attention to the mechanisms of accountability is a little bit like having the generals design the standards with which the troops march into battle but not caring very much about what weapons they plan to deploy.

Roswell Perkins: I think we should give Margaret the final word.

Margaret Blair: I just want to take on one issue. It wasn't my intention to put forth in the book a new paradigm or a new duty that would have the force of law. It *was* my intention, however, to create a new duty or at least to ensure a broader range of discretion for directors. And my thought when I wrote the book was that it should be a moral duty. I think social norms do matter in these things. I would impose a moral duty on directors and managers to take into account the effect of their decisions on all of the parties that have firm-specific investments at risk. And the more I hear from the lawyers, the more I am convinced that, under the law, they probably have the discretion to do this now.

What does it mean to have a moral duty, and is that duty enforceable? It can potentially create all kinds of problems. But that is why the kind of thing that Ron Gilson is talking about is important. Maybe it's possible to create the functional effect you want by getting your distribution of equity shares right. If managers and directors began to think in these terms, it might help them begin to think creatively about how to deal with the problems that arise when they have a company whose costs are too high and they need to get them under

control. How do they change the system in a way that reallo-
cates risk and reward and acknowledges that firm-specific
capital is at risk, not all of which was contributed by shareholders?

Notes

1. See Margaret M. Blair, "Corporate Ownership: A Misleading Word Muddies the Corporate Governance Debate," *Brookings Review,* Winter 1995, pp. 16–19.

2. Robert C. Topel, "Specific Capital, Mobility, and Wages: Wages Rise with Job Seniority," *Journal of Political Economy,* 99, no. 1 (February 1991), pp. 145–76.

3. Technically, the economic surplus generated by the firm's activities consists of "rents" and "quasi rents." Rents are returns that exceed the long-run return that the relevant resources could be earning if those resources were used in their next best way. Quasi rents are returns that exceed the short-run return that the resources could earn in their next best use. Fixed assets that cannot be readily redeployed can earn large quasi rents, even when they are earning no real rents. Nevertheless, once an investment has been made in such fixed assets, the economic return earned by those assets includes both the rents and the quasi rents.

4. Author's calculations based on data from U.S. Congress, Joint Economic Committee, *The 1995 Economic Report of the President* (1995), table B-13.

5. Paul Milgrom and John Roberts note that "two assets are cospecialized if they are most productive when used together and lose much of

their value if used separately to produce independent products or services." See *Economics, Organization and Management* (Prentice Hall, 1992), p. 135.

6. A classic example of this sort of reasoning carried to its extreme appears in an article by Michael Jensen that argues that, because General Motors failed to make a competitive return on its investments in the 1980s (based on the performance of its stock price relative to a benchmark rate of return), society would have been better off if the company had made no investments, but had instead returned all of its cash flow to shareholders. See "The Modern Industrial Revolution, Exit, and the Failure of Internal Control Systems," *Journal of Finance*, 48, no. 3 (July 1993), pp. 831–80.

7. Robert E. Hall, "Employment Fluctuations and Wage Rigidities," *Brookings Papers on Economic Activity*, 1: 1980, pp. 90–123.

8. See Topel, "Specific Capital, Mobility, and Wages," tables 1, 3.

9. Kenneth A. Swinnerton and Howard Wial, "Is Job Stability Declining in the U.S. Economy?" *Industrial and Labor Relations Review*, 48 (January 1995), pp. 293–304.

10. A paper by Francis X. Diebold, David Neumark, and Daniel Polsky, "Job Stability in the United States," Working Paper 4859 (Cambridge, Mass.: National Bureau of Economic Research, September 1994), relying on the same *Census Population Surveys* as Swinnerton and Wial, confirms a drop in retention probabilities for high school–educated workers with neither very short nor very long tenure, but fails to find such a drop for college-educated workers. An analysis of the two results by Dave E. Marcotte, "Declining Job Stability: What We Know and What It Means," *Journal of Policy Analysis and Management* (Fall 1995), pp. 590–98, pinpoints the source of the difference in the technical adjustments made by Diebold *et al.* to try to eliminate some shortcomings in the data. The validity of these adjustments is difficult to prove or disprove. My reading of this and related evidence leads me to believe that the drop in tenure and retention probabilities is real, but that its magnitude is uncertain.

11. See Oliver Hart, *Firms, Contracts and Financial Structure* (Oxford University Press, 1995).

12. Data are from internal reports, Office of Research of the Pension Welfare and Benefits Administration, U.S. Department of Labor.

13. See U.S. Department of Labor, Office of the American Workplace, "High Performance Work Practices and Firm Performance" (August, 1993); and Sarah C. Mavrinac and Neil R. Jones, "The Financial

and Nonfinancial Returns to Innovative Workplace Practices: A Critical Review," report prepared for the U.S. Department of Labor, Office of the American Workforce (undated).

14. See U.S. Department of Labor, Office of the American Workplace, "Guide to Responsible Restructuring," (Washington, 1995), pp. 5–6.

15. In 1985, IBM acquired Rolm Corp., an entrepreneurial telecommunications equipment manufacturer, for $1.5 billion. IBM reportedly promised Rolm managers and staff that they would be given autonomy and that their corporate culture would be preserved. Within one year, however, losses began to mount at Rolm, and "IBM absorbed Rolm into its legendary bureaucracy, closed Rolm plants and forced it to hire transferred IBMers. Top Rolm managers quit. IBM, in its hubris, thought it could run the unfamiliar business without them," according to the *Wall Street Journal*. "In 1988, IBM sold off Rolm to Siemens AG for about $350 million less than it had originally paid." See Bart Ziegler, "Corporate Focus: IBM's History Raises Doubts about Lotus Acquisition; Some Wonder If Company This Time Can Keep Vows while Integrating Notes," *Wall Street Journal*, June 14, 1995, p. B6.

16. General Motors acquired computer services company EDS in 1984 for $2.5 billion, creating a special class of General Motors stock, Class E, to give to EDS shareholders (including EDS founder Ross Perot and a large number of other EDS employees) as part of the transaction.

17. In 1986, following a public dispute between Ross Perot and GM chairman Roger B. Smith over how EDS should be run, GM bought out Perot's holdings of Class E stock for $743 million as part of a deal to remove Perot from the GM board. Press accounts of that incident noted that GM officials "recognize that they made a fundamental error in granting 'substantial independence'" to EDS. "The mistake allowed [Perot] to continue running the company as if he still owned it," and "encouraged EDS to charge GM high prices" for its services. See Warren Brown, "GM's Big Mistake Rooted in Perot's Grant of Freedom," *Washington Post,* December 9, 1986, p. D9. In 1995, GM announced that it would split off EDS as an independent company again. See Robert L. Simison, "GM Moves ahead on EDS Spinoff; But Plan to Distribute $22.31 Billion of Stock Hinges on IRS Ruling," *Wall Street Journal*, August 8, 1995.

18. American Law Institute, *Principles of Corporate Governance: Analysis and Recommendations,* vol. 1, §. 2.01 at 55 (St. Paul, Minn.,1994).

19. Margaret Blair, *Ownership and Control: Rethinking Corporate Governance for the Twenty-First Century* (Brookings, 1995), p. 235.

20. Ibid., p. 219.

21. Ibid., p. 239.

22. Ibid., p. 326.

23. For an excellent elaboration of these ideas see Robert Charles Clark, *Corporate Law* (Boston: Little, Brown, 1986), pp. 17–18.

24. See *Tomorrow's Company: the Role of Business in the Changing World* (London: Royal Society for the Encouragement of Arts, Manufactures and Commerce, 1995).

25. See Robert A. G. Monks and Nell Minow, *Corporate Governance* (Cambridge, Mass.: Blackwell Business, 1995).

26. Saatchi & Saatchi was founded in 1970 by two brothers and, during the 1980s, went public and acquired numerous other advertising agencies to build one of the largest advertising companies in the world. In the process the firm accumulated a significant amount of debt. Under pressure from banks and shareholders, the Saatchi brothers brought in an outside management team in 1989. By 1993 conflicts between the Saatchis and Charles Scott, a financial executive who had by then been made chief executive officer, became intense. By early 1994 three institutional investors that held large blocks of Saatchi & Saatchi stock began plotting to have one of the brothers, Maurice Saatchi, removed from the company. They succeeded by the end of 1994. In early 1995 Saatchi & Saatchi's stock price began falling. Amid a flurry of lawsuits and countersuits, Maurice Saatchi, along with several former Saatchi & Saatchi executives, formed a new advertising agency. The original Saatchi & Saatchi, with its stock price down 40 percent by March 1995, was forced to change its name (to Cordiant PLC) to dissociate itself from the turmoil. See "Inside Out: Saatchi's Implosion: Tale of Power and Ego across Two Continents; How the Huge Ad Agency Found Itself under Siege and Facing a New Rival; A Strong Signal from Mars," *Wall Street Journal*, January 12, 1995, p. A1; Kyle Pope and Tara Parker-Pope, "Marketing and Media: Saatchi Loses Effort in Court to Block Ex-Chairman's Plan for Rival Agency," *Wall Street Journal*, February 14, 1995, p. B12; and "Marketing and Media: Saatchi's New Name," *Wall Street Journal*, March 17, 1995, p. B7.

27. American Law Institute, *Principles of Corporate Governance*, p. 55.

28. Ibid., comment to §. 2.01 at 56, Reporter's Note to §. 2.01 at 73.